W9-BXT-255

ILLINOIS CENTRAL COLLEGE

2

A12901 771589

6/09

I.C.C. LIBRARY

DEMCO

Prostitution

Other Books in the Social Issues Firsthand Series:

Prostitution

Ronnie D. Lankford Jr., Book Editor

GREENHAVEN PRESS
A part of Gale, Cengage Learning

I.C.C. LIBRARY

GALE
CENGAGE Learning™

Detroit • New York • San Francisco • New Haven, Conn • Waterville, Maine • London

HQ
118
.P765
2008

GALE
CENGAGE Learning

Christine Nasso, *Publisher*
Elizabeth Des Chenes, *Managing Editor*

© 2008 Greenhaven Press, a part of Gale, Cengage Learning

For more information, contact:
Greenhaven Press
27500 Drake Rd.
Farmington Hills, MI 48331-3535
Or you can visit our Internet site at gale.cengage.com

ALL RIGHTS RESERVED
No part of this work covered by the copyright herein may be reproduced, transmitted, stored, or used in any form or by any means graphic, electronic, or mechanical, including but not limited to photocopying, recording, scanning, digitizing, taping, Web distribution, information networks, or information storage retrieval systems, except as permitted under Section 107 or 108 of the 1976 United States Copyright Act, without the prior written permission of the publisher.

For product information and technology assistance, contact us at

Gale Customer Support, 1-800-877-4253
For permission to use material from this text or product, submit all requests online at www.cengage.com/permissions

Further permissions questions can be emailed to permissionrequest@cengage.com

Articles in Greenhaven Press anthologies are often edited for length to meet page requirements. In addition, original titles of these works are changed to clearly present the main thesis and to explicitly indicate the author's opinion. Every effort is made to ensure that Greenhaven Press accurately reflects the original intent of the authors. Every effort has been made to trace the owners of copyrighted material.

Cover photograph reproduced by permission of image copyright Igor Balasanov, 2008. Used under license from Shutterstock.com.

LIBRARY OF CONGRESS CATALOGING-IN-PUBLICATION DATA

Prostitution / Ronnie D. Lankford, book editor.
   p. cm. -- (Social issues firsthand)
  Includes bibliographical references and index.
  ISBN-13: 978-0-7377-4136-0 (hardcover)
  1. Prostitution. 2. Feminism. I. Lankford, Ronald D., 1962-
  HQ118.P765 2008
  363.4'4--dc22

                                                 2008009621

Printed in the United States of America
1 2 3 4 5 6 7 12 11 10 09 08

Contents

1/09 B&T 29.95

Foreword

Social issues are often viewed in abstract terms. Pressing challenges such as poverty, homelessness, and addiction are viewed as problems to be defined and solved. Politicians, social scientists, and other experts engage in debates about the extent of the problems, their causes, and how best to remedy them. Often overlooked in these discussions is the human dimension of the issue. Behind every policy debate over poverty, homelessness, and substance abuse, for example, are real people struggling to make ends meet, to survive life on the streets, and to overcome addiction to drugs and alcohol. Their stories are ubiquitous and compelling. They are the stories of everyday people—perhaps your own family members or friends—and yet they rarely influence the debates taking place in state capitols, the national Congress, or the courts.

The disparity between the public debate and private experience of social issues is well illustrated by looking at the topic of poverty. Each year the U.S. Census Bureau establishes a poverty threshold. A household with an income below the threshold is defined as poor, while a household with an income above the threshold is considered able to live on a basic subsistence level. For example, in 2003 a family of two was considered poor if its income was less than $12,015; a family of four was defined as poor if its income was less than $18,810. Based on this system, the bureau estimates that 35.9 million Americans (12.5 percent of the population) lived below the poverty line in 2003, including 12.9 million children below the age of eighteen.

Commentators disagree about what these statistics mean. Social activists insist that the huge number of officially poor Americans translates into human suffering. Even many families that have incomes above the threshold, they maintain, are likely to be struggling to get by. Other commentators insist that the statistics exaggerate the problem of poverty in the United States. Compared to people in developing countries, they point out, most so-called poor families have a high quality of life. As stated by journalist Fidelis Iyebote, "Cars are owned by 70 percent of 'poor' households. . . . Color televisions belong to 97 percent of the 'poor' [and] videocassette recorders belong to nearly 75 percent. . . . Sixty-four percent have microwave ovens, half own a stereo system, and over a quarter possess an automatic dishwasher."

However, this debate over the poverty threshold and what it means is likely irrelevant to a person living in poverty. Simply put, poor people do not need the government to tell them whether they are poor. They can see it in the stack of bills they cannot pay. They are aware of it when they are forced to choose between paying rent or buying food for their children. They become painfully conscious of it when they lose their homes and are forced to live in their cars or on the streets. Indeed, the written stories of poor people define the meaning of poverty more vividly than a government bureaucracy could ever hope to. Narratives composed by the poor describe losing jobs due to injury or mental illness, depict horrific tales of childhood abuse and spousal violence, recount the loss of friends and family members. They evoke the slipping away of social supports and government assistance, the descent into substance abuse and addiction, the harsh realities of life on the streets. These are the perspectives on poverty that are too often omitted from discussions over the extent of the problem and how to solve it.

Greenhaven Press's Social Issues Firsthand series provides a forum for the often-overlooked human perspectives on society's most divisive topics of debate. Each volume focuses on one social issue and presents a collection of ten to sixteen narratives by those who have had personal involvement with the topic. Extra care has been taken to include a diverse range of perspectives. For example, in the volume on adoption, readers will find the stories of birth parents who have made an adoption plan, adoptive parents, and adoptees themselves. After exposure to these varied points of view, the reader will have a clearer understanding that adoption is an intense, emotional experience full of joyous highs and painful lows for all concerned.

The debate surrounding embryonic stem cell research illustrates the moral and ethical pressure that the public brings to bear on the scientific community. However, while nonexperts often criticize scientists for not considering the potential negative impact of their work, ironically the public's reaction against such discoveries can produce harmful results as well. For example, although the outcry against embryonic stem cell research in the United States has resulted in fewer embryos being destroyed, those with Parkinson's, such as actor Michael J. Fox, have argued that prohibiting the development of new stem cell lines ultimately will prevent a timely cure for the disease that is killing Fox and thousands of others.

Each book in the series contains several features that enhance its usefulness, including an in-depth introduction, an annotated table of contents, bibliographies for further research, a list of organizations to contact, and a thorough index. These elements—combined with the poignant voices of people touched by tragedy and triumph—make the Social Issues Firsthand series a valuable resource for research on today's topics of political discussion.

Introduction

It is a familiar cliché that prostitution is the world's oldest profession. But exactly who works in the profession is often obscured by the illegality of prostitution along with the prevalence of stereotypes in television and movies. Streetwalkers and high-class call girls have long been staples of police dramas, but these stereotypes only represent a limited number of persons working within prostitution.

Likewise, many people assume that all prostitutes are women, all originate from the lower classes, and all have been abused as children. In truth, both men and women are prostitutes, and they come from every social class, family background, and racial group. Some are men or women facing economic hard times, students paying for college, or single middle-class parents striving to pay the mortgage and send their child to private school. Prostitution, then, is not only the oldest profession, but also one of the most varied.

While the familiar "hooker" who walks the street looking for a "John" (a customer) is visible, much of prostitution remains hidden. Liaisons are arranged by telephone, CB radio, and e-mail, and business is conducted in hotels, apartments, and parking lots. The following descriptions offer a brief overview of the most varied of professions.

While "call girls" continue to exist, the term "escort" is more commonly used today. The escort may work independently or for an escort service. If the escort works independently, the escort will place a coded advertisement in a magazine, newspaper, or on the Internet to solicit clients. If a call girl works for an escort service, then the escort service arranges the meetings and also receives a percentage of the transaction. Generally speaking, escorts are younger and receive more for their services than men and women who work in street prostitution. Many also believe that working as an escort is safer than many forms of prostitution. Despite the illegality of exchanging sex for money, many escort services operate openly: as long as the advertised services never state that sex is being exchanged for money, then these agencies are allowed to exist in a legal gray area. The man or woman from the agency simply accompanies (escorts) the client at his or her convenience.

With street prostitution, the prostitute (most frequently a woman) literally walks the street and waits for customers to solicit her services. As with escorting, some street prostitutes work independently, while others work with pimps who manage their work and receive a percentage of the exchange. Generally, working as a street prostitute is considered dangerous and unsanitary, and many of these workers also use illegal drugs (some people become prostitutes to earn drug money). Johns sometimes abuse street prostitutes, and working as a street prostitute is physically demanding. While an escort may potentially exchange his or her services to a small number of clients for several hundred dollars per hour, street prostitutes often earn little per transaction, forcing him or her to seek many customers. Despite the many disadvantages, street prostitution offers independence to workers, and has drawn many prostitutes who once worked in brothels and as escorts.

Sex tourism is a branch of the sex trade set up in many countries to accommodate tourists and businesspersons from other countries. Often, the travelers come from wealthier countries (the United States, Europe, and Japan, for instance) to partake in sexual activities in less-prosperous countries (Thailand, Brazil, and Costa Rica, for instance). Frequently, a business will garner favor with a client or reward an employee by sending him on a sex tour in a foreign country. Sex tourism is controversial because underage girls are commonly exploited by the sex tourism industry, and some prostitutes may be working against their will. Because of the frequent exploitation, the United Nations opposes sex tourism. Domestic sex tourism takes place when people travel within their own country to visit a location where prostitution is legal (as with Nevada in the United States).

Brothels, also referred to as bordellos, are residences that house prostitutes. In a number of counties in Nevada in the United States, brothels remain legal, the most famous being the Mustang Ranch, which is no longer in operation. Another famous brothel in the United States was the illegal Chicken Ranch in La Grange, Texas, which served as the basis for the 1982 movie, *Best Little Whorehouse in Texas*. Brothels, like prostitution itself, can be traced to ancient Greek society, and traveling brothels have often served as adjunct units to armies. Some countries that have legalized prostitution (e.g., Germany and New Zealand) favor the establishment of brothels as a way of curtailing the abuses of street prostitutes.

Prostitution includes a number of subcategories that are only known among the people who employ their services. "Lot Lizards," for example, are prostitutes who meet with truck drivers. The prostitute may advertise over a CB radio, and then arrange to meet the truck driver at a parking lot or a rest stop. In Russia, an outdoor market for prostitution is known as a "tochka." As with sex tourism, there has been a great deal of concern that many Russian prostitutes are minors, and that others are working as prostitutes against their will. The definition of who is and is not a prostitute is also very fluid, especially within the broader field of sex work. Men and women who work as exotic dancers and within the pornography industry may choose to earn extra money in prostitution, or simply work as a prostitute when other work is unavailable.

Prostitution permeates society in the United States and abroad. Escort services are advertised on the Internet, and a number of escorts maintain blogs describing escorting experiences. Prostitution is also common in "red light" districts in major cities around the world, like Achterdam in the city of

Alkmaar in the Netherlands, and parts of the SoHo area in London's West End. Many ex-prostitutes have written "tell all" memoirs that have landed on the best seller list, while other ex-prostitutes have worked to extract other men and women who remain in the profession. There are unions that work to preserve the rights of prostitutes, and law enforcement officials who attempt to shut prostitution rings down.

Despite legal, moral, and health issues, prostitution seems to be a permanent part of the social landscape in both the United States and around the world. Although restrictions exist, prostitution is legal in many European countries and continues to be tolerated in many countries where it remains illegal. The entrenched nature of the world's oldest profession, then, assures that citizens will continue to grapple with the social impact of prostitution for the foreseeable future.

The Many Facets
of Prostitution

I Was a Teenage Prostitute

Lisa Carver

*For a brief period of her life, performance artist Lisa Carver de-
cided to become a prostitute. While some of her experiences were
negative, she generally liked being a prostitute. She enjoyed playing various roles and having the power to make her customers
happy. The women she worked with, however, seemed worn
down by prostitution, and all—except her—were on drugs. While
Carver liked being able to disappear into her role as a prostitute,
she eventually left the profession to regain her "own life and
body" back. Carver wrote a popular, 'zine titled* Rollerderby
*during the early 1990s and was a member of the band Suckdog.
She published her experiences as a prostitute in* Drugs Are Nice:
A Post Punk Memoir.

When I tell Jean Louis over the phone upon my return to
America that I've decided to become a prostitute, he
says: "You risk your health, your life?"

"No, no," I tell him. "It's safe. They have a bouncer. It's in
a parlor." I found it in the phonebook, under Massage Parlors.
I called all the places listed until one of the people answering
didn't ask me if I was "licensed." He used a tone both guarded
and insinuating, finally asking if I wanted to come "audition."

I've wanted to be a prostitute for as long as I can remember. I've wanted to be Rhett's warm, wisecracking prostitute
friend in *Gone With the Wind*, not Scarlett—she had better
makeup, velvety-er clothes. Prostitutes fight with all the girls
who don't enter their little gang, their faction (and the prostitutes always win!), and they make cold, sad men come alive.
Perhaps becoming a prostitute will arm me, too, with zinging
comebacks and a hidden, smart tenderness.

Lisa Carver, *Drugs Are Nice: A Post Punk Memoir*, Soft Skull Press, Brooklyn, NY:
2005. Copyright © 2005 Lisa Crystal Carver. Reprinted by permission of the publisher.

Jean Louis writes that he understands that I'm "nineteen, walking bitch and beautiful down thin time, like thin panty between your stalking legs." Did he mean "stocking-ed legs?" I choose "stalking!" Everyone in my family is pretty ugly. I don't have great bone structure or anything—you can tell already I'm going to be tired-looking when I'm older. It's pure youth and sexfulness that I possess, mixed with fear and pleasure. The mess of it all quivers on my skin and in my walk. When I catch my reflection in a store window, it stops me dead in my tracks! I know this beauty belongs to nineteen, not to me. It feels like it was given to me by mistake, and its rightful owner will return at any moment. I want to really do something with it, while I have it. The operatic shows I've been doing are too confusing and repulsive for anyone to see what I actually look like. And I can't be a dancer because I have no rhythm. I'd like to be an acrobat, but I'm not strong enough. Looks like being a prostitute is the only option.

Becoming a Prostitute

I stare out the window on the long ride up I-95 to the little brick cathouse. The last leaf has fallen, and the trees are once again frozen silver lightning bolts rising up out of the ground. It's a new world.

I meet my first trick mere days before turning twenty. He's at least sixty years old. Maybe seventy. Maybe eighty! He shakes off the cold and pays the first hundred dollars in the little "office" that the front door immediately opens into (I believe it was the foyer, when a family formerly lived here). He enters the big-screen-TV room, where a half-dozen of us bra-and-pantied or bathing-suit-and-pantyhosed ladies sit around waiting. (I'm in a black and crimson contraption that looks like tangled kite string with no kite.) We shift into our "pick me!" poses. Mine entails sitting up straight, like a meerkat. The more beautiful the girl, the less she poses. Candy, who looks like a perfect plastic doll, practically turns her back on the poor old man. He lifts his hand sort of in my direction, so I leap up and show him where the showers are, down in the basement, like I'd been taught in my ten-minute "training session." Then I show him where my hot, tiny room is, and ask him to meet me there after his shower.

A previous occupant taped a piece of lavender tissue paper over my ceiling's rectangular fluorescent light. A framed poster of a Corvette is shiny under glass, looking ready to take off. My old man, moist from his shower, comes in and lays down on the rickety "massage table" on his back, his towel falling partly open. He seems a little embarrassed and a little joyful. I watch in the wall-size mirror in disbelief as I move confidently across his mass of soft, furry, Silly Putty skin. An hour or so later, he pauses, in his unbuttoned shirt and unbelted pants, considering. He reaches into his wallet and pulls out an extra hundred, on top of the hundred he already put on the table, "for being so sweet."

As soon as the old man and I emerge from that room, another man comes in and points to me. This one looks just like Frankenstein. Candy squeezes my hand. I try to show him the showers but he refuses. Meekly, I reenter my room, and Frankenstein closes the door behind us. He's big. "They're going to hear us," he says. I can't tell from his expression whether he's pleased about that or not. I wonder what he has in mind that will be so noisy.

"They don't care," I say.

"Of course they don't," sneers Frankenstein. "They're *whores*. Get undressed."

I comply. He stares hard at my naked body, which I nervously try to cover before realizing how silly that is in this situation. He asks me if this is my first night, and I say yes.

"I mean, this your first time? You never fuck any of your boyfriends? How old are you—sixteen?"

I nod.

"Liar," he growls. "Get down on the ground."

After it's over, he takes two twenties and a ten out of his wallet and lets them flutter down onto my body. "Always get your money first, little girl," he grins. "Not all guys are as nice as me."

The Life of a Prostitute

Frankenstein is not the only creep ever to pick me, but he is the only one I don't know how to handle. Quickly, I get as wisecracking and as slippery as my childhood fantasy prostitute—but only with someone trying to put something over on me. Most of my clients are great. . . . I love joking with Candy and Sandy—who is getting on in years and gets back at me for having more clients than her by slyly dumping small amounts of cigarette ash in my room after I vacuum and then telling Carl, our pimp, that I didn't vacuum at all. I love rolling my eyes at Carl, who wears a cowboy hat and dyes his gray hair black and strums a guitar. Most of all I love my time in the little room under the engine-racing Corvette poster.

I get to change my personality five times a night, stepping into other people's ideals. I can guess—from a man's greeting, from his clothes, his eyes—who his dream woman is, and I become her. I take on her bearing, her speech, her interests. It's a lot like my shows, except I don't have to come up with my own character or new rhymes. The men's fantasies aren't particularly unique: one wants a dominatrix, one a naive girl, one a sophisticated companion, one a filthy slut, one a kind ear. Even the dialogue men respond to . . . is canned: "You've been a bad, bad boy." "I've been a very bad girl." "Put your money on the table and shut your mouth." "Oh really—Alaska? Tell me everything!" But to say all those things sincerely, to be that person for twenty minutes . . . to zing from one personality to another . . . this brings me happiness, in the same way the shows do; escape from awareness of self. Unlike touring, though, it also brings me thousands of dollars a week.

Though I'm happy, sadness is in the air. All the girls but me are on drugs. While I occasionally indulge in my time off, I don't want my vision clouded while on the job. I am curious about the people who would come to a prostitute, or be a boyfriend to a prostitute and pick her up at the end of her shift and take her home. I soberly watch everything and everyone, including myself. All the girls but me have been here a long time. I can see that it gets hard after a while—or at least very weird—to live inside other people's dreams. In Candy's case, she literally lives, and drives, off of other people's use of her beauty. Her sporty little car and her spacious, bright apartment are both paid for with one-hour sessions each month, to the car dealer and the landlord. The drugs are always gifts, or trades, as well. Along with hundred-dollar restaurant meals and concert tickets. Prostitution isolates you, with all its little ways that people not in it don't understand, much in the way some religions do, or drug addictions. It's hard to explain certain things, and after a while it's easier to not talk to anyone outside much at all. I thought that as a prostitute, I would no longer be inside a dream; I'd be flung, newly sharp and capable, into life. Actually, I discover, the opposite is true. Prostitution is a complex, shared dream where everyone agrees to not wake up, for just a little longer. . . .

[My work as a prostitute affects] how I have sex these days: it feels like bringing my work home. I can't even masturbate. It feels too quiet. I need that third party now: me, the person I'm with, and the person I imagine they are imagining. Sex for me—after only a few months on the job!—is only about becoming. I no longer know what I am when there aren't strangers around whose minds I can read and holograph myself into. I feel downright ridiculous having sex just as me! At first, I was hiding my personality at will. Now I think I'm actually losing it. I buy a ticket for France. I have to quit my job because I like it too much.

No one still "in life" will talk about it, and it seems like those who left will only talk about the bad side. But as I walk away from prostitution and drug addicts and gain back my own life and body, I know I'm losing something too. I lose nothingness. I lose the concealed passageway I found into other people's something-ness. The lights in the airport are so white! I'm not even on the plane yet, and already I miss everything I'm leaving behind: the somber lighting, the camaraderie with the girls, everyone being awake with you while the rest of the world sleeps. I miss the drifting conversation of people who are high. I miss my clients; I miss being on top and being nothing, being only what I can see in their eyes, always new.

Lots of underground front-women strip: Jennifer from Royal Trux, Kathleen Hanna from Bikini Kill, Courtney Love—just tons of them! None of them admit to being an out-and-out prostitute, but I hear some are. Did they, like me, want to squeeze all they could out of the mantle of beauty they found by surprise around their shoulders one morning?

Someone on [1990s-era talk show] *Jenny Jones* said that seventy percent of girls abandoned by their fathers turn to promiscuity and drugs. If fifty percent of our parents divorced, and ninety percent of the mothers got custody, that would at least look like abandonment to ninety percent of fifty percent—and seventy percent of that equals thirty-one point five percent. So, one out of three—that's how many of us Gen X girls, according to my calculations, should have turned out slutty drug dabblers.

I think Jenny Jones should add "really creative" to that set of descriptors. My reading of art history books tells me that abandonment has always led to advanced creativity. The greatest periods of art flowering have also been the most precarious periods for children. In Greece, when the arts, politics, and philosophies were exploding, inconvenient babies were regularly "exposed"—left to die. And then in the Renaissance

. . . well, let's look at Michelangelo and Da Vinci. Michelangelo was sent off to a wet nurse as soon as he was born, and didn't see his mother again till he was two; then she went and died on him when he was six. Da Vinci was a love child who was given up at the age of four by his peasant mother when his rich father married. Freud describes Mona Lisa's smile as holding "the promise of unbounded tenderness and at the same time sinister menace." That's how Da Vinci looked at all women after being abandoned by one. I know for me, my father's smile, and everything he says, is nothing if not a double-edged promise. Prostitution—and promiscuity, and weird sex, and the shows, with their combination of flirting and hurting people and shifting reality—are chances to turn things around, for me to give that promise back.

I Am a Prostitute and a Writer

Belle de Jour

Although Belle de Jour (her name has been borrowed from a 1967 movie about a housewife who assumes Belle de Jour as a pseudonym when she begins to work as a prostitute) never planned to become a prostitute, she entered the profession because she needed money. She denies that the work is undignified, however, or that all prostitutes come from abusive or impoverished backgrounds. In her case, she grew up a precocious child of liberal parents, spending her spare time reading everything from classic literature to the autobiography of pornography star Linda Lovelace. Belle de Jour admits that it is difficult to have a boyfriend while working as a prostitute, and that she has kept her profession a secret from her family. Eventually, Belle de Jour decided to share her experience in the form of a written journal, reminding readers that women can be both sexually active and intelligent.

My alarm is never set; I rise at a different hour each day. I eat breakfast, check my e-mail and update the weblog—little chores. My working day proper begins at four or five in the afternoon when I shower and dress. The first meeting, unless I have a lunch date, is usually at seven. Sometimes there's only one; sometimes more. Occasionally I work all night and come home at 7am.

I always ring someone when I arrive at a job and again when I leave—on longer assignments, once every few hours. The manager tends to worry when she doesn't hear from me. She used to have my job, too.

Just so you know—I'm a whore. Not in the metaphorical sense, often invoked by writers my age, of auctioning my in-

Belle de Jour, "I Am a Young Woman. I Have Sex for Money. And I Love to Write. This Is My Story. . . .," *Daily Telegraph*, March, 2004. Reproduced by permission.

tellectual abilities to the highest bidder. I'm not some disillusioned twentysomething desk-job graduate equating salaried work with selling out. No, I'm an actual, exchanging-money-for-sex prostitute.

It's been my job for almost a year, and while it's unlikely to be a long-term career move, I'm not gagging to get out of it either. Work is good. The pay is great. Job satisfaction is high. I never felt this positive working in a bookshop. Of course, it's not for everyone. (Then again, neither is accountancy, though my friends seem to be moving over to it at a depressing rate.) It's not even for a remotely significant percentage of the population—and truth be told, I've met more than a few women on the game who should not have been there. It's no cinematic fantasy of bubble baths and Lotus drivers, but nor is it the abject horror of being a streetwalker. It's hotel visits. It's near-anonymous sex. It's learning to have no qualms or hesitation about the 'latex moment'. It's one first date after another where the man always scores.

An Accidental Profession

I always loved sex, always enjoyed meeting people. Even before I began this job there were plenty of mornings when I woke up and wondered who on earth that was next to me and where my knickers were. I'd shower and dress, stay for the obligatory polite cup of tea, then wander back out into the world—blinking at the sun, dressed in the previous night's clothes. This job doesn't feel different from that. If anything, it's better. No one feels obliged to ring the day after.

As a student I did other sex-related work; the summer after I began university I worked as a stripper. That was my first experience of how strange men can be. They didn't seem to find it odd to discuss [Chilean writer] Pablo Neruda with a topless woman as a preface to a lap-dance, but I did. I couldn't stop giggling and eventually offended too many customers. The manager had to let me go, but I didn't mind—term was starting again anyway.

A year later I was at a party talking to a professional dominatrix. She liked my poise, she said; she liked the way I laughed. Would I be interested in a little work on the side? So I bought the customary PVC [vinyl] dresses and dusted off the riding-crop—but again, it was difficult to take seriously. It's hard to keep your nerve when a man in big white girly pants is cleaning your stilettos with his tongue. When I left—more due to lack of interest than a better offer—I didn't imagine getting into sex work again.

It happened. The usual story: impoverished graduate in depressing London bedsit [apartment] seeks career with integrity or, failing that, a fat pay-cheque. Temp work is depressing and poorly paid. By comparison the money in escorting—up to £300 per hour—was irresistible. With one appointment a week I covered my bills. Two a week and I could eat out. Three and I could afford new clothes. A slippery slope, you might say.

The Diverse Background of Prostitutes

People ask what in my background could possibly have led to this and I'm not sure what to say. My family doesn't fit the profile of your average whore's upbringing. I am not the victim of childhood sexual abuse or a chronic lack of attention from my parents. No one believes me, of course; as we all know, sexual promiscuity is necessarily the result of low self-esteem or some such rubbish.

I disagree. I've met other prostitutes and, yes, many are drug addicts, survivors of abuse, or both. Some hate it from day one, but persist because they know no other way to support themselves. But a few are like me—a bit in debt but not unemployable.

It's a useful stopgap.

Having seen so many people naked is a great equaliser. Clothes off, it doesn't matter what someone drives or does for a living. I feel comfortable that way, competent around bodies. I know I don't look it. Clients often treat me exceptionally gently at first, as if I might break, and it is a large part of the job to egg them into a frenzy. At my interview with the escort agency, the manager worried about my squeamishness. Perhaps I don't look very robust.

'Will you be OK with the work, even if the man is perhaps not very handsome?' she asked in her thick eastern European accent.

'Of course,' I said. Why, did other girls demand they only be assigned film stars?

'And you know, some of the men, they like very strange things,' she said cautiously.

'I like strange things, too,' I assured her, remembering the former boyfriend who had an uncomfortable afternoon explaining the pulleys in the ceiling when his parents came to visit. While he squirmed and avoided their questions I just smiled and put the kettle on.

'I can handle it,' I said.

Maybe there was something else about me she distrusted. When we arrived at the restaurant she insisted on a window table and looked constantly over her shoulder. Maybe she suspected me of trying to trap her; exchanging sex for money is not illegal in Britain, but being a madame is. 'I had to let a girl go recently,' she confided. 'She was too much a feminist, if you know what I mean.'

I knew what she meant, but don't think the concepts are incompatible.

Childhood Influences

My parents fancied themselves 1970s revolutionaries so we grew up with unfettered access to the writings of [activist] Angela Davis, [feminist] Germaine Greer et al. The house was stuffed with books of all kinds. Psychedelic sci-fi disguised as literature: Aldous Huxley. The usual classics: [The writings of Benedictine monk] Bede, *Ivanhoe* [by Sir Walter Scott]. My parents claim I taught myself to read, and set about reading everything within reach. Euripides [Greek playwright] and Plato [Greek philosopher] were bedside standards. [German authors] Goethe and Grass were favourites. Those done with, there was only one book left in the house. It was the only thing my parents ever tried to hide from their children. There was a drawer of things they wanted out of reach of small hands. It wasn't locked—we worked on a trust system in the family. I mostly respected this, because all the drawer usually contained was the recreational drugs I wasn't supposed to know about and completely lacked interest in. But when I noticed the bookshelves were subtly rearranged one day I headed straight for the drawer. I found the book with its Mills & Boon-style cover sitting on top of an Indian box containing decades-old hash.

It was Linda Lovelace's autobiography, *Ordeal*. I didn't know who she was, but was fascinated by this tale of a slightly wayward girl taken advantage of. And because when you are that young masturbation is a hungry devourer of images, regardless of their origin, her book fuelled many heated fantasies involving a hairdryer and [American entertainer] Sammy Davis Jr. When my mother found the book in my laundry basket she sighed, saw that I had already finished it, and returned it to the bookshelf in full view.

Masturbation took up a lot of spare time that year. But not just that; I'd also imagine conversations with suitors before the act itself, and play out (with a conveniently placed pillow) the denouement of the lovemaking. Maybe I have an overactive imagination, because one time I actually had a postcoital argument with the pillow; we spent the entire night on opposite sides of the bed. And I knew years before having sex what I would most like done to me. Nothing big. I just wanted someone to kiss the skin of my arm between the shoulder and bicep. I can kiss it myself, of course, but that's not the same. Actually, I still want someone to do this spontaneously; no one ever has.

Years later someone told me that Lovelace's entire book had been discredited, that she wasn't raped, that it was all a lie. But if even one tenth of the things she described were real, then I feel very sorry for her indeed. To gain sexual knowledge at the expense of your self-esteem seems an unfair trade.

Growing Up

When I was five or six my parents' friends started to call me the 'Little Alice'. As in, through the looking-glass. 'Where is the Little Alice?' they'd ask, and I'd run from wherever I was, eager to please. I was brought out at gatherings to impress with prodigious feats of memorisation. I knew they were patronising me but I liked talking back to them in their own language. One family friend refused to dine at our table if not seated next to me. He asked what I thought about politics, and was surprised to learn I had opinions—however uninformed. (This really hasn't changed much since.) Then he asked me to recite poetry, going over [poet Philip] Larkin's 'The Whitsun Weddings' with me line by line, showing where the ironic pauses and dry humour should be. I recited it back verbatim. 'Some day you might even absorb all this,' he laughed.

Sometimes during the summer holidays my mother would leave me with a Jewish youth group. Usually we'd play board games or strange sports no one knew the rules of, like korfball. Sometimes we took trips. We went to the beach in two minibuses; the sand got everywhere. When we came back the adults ordered the girls and boys into separate rooms to change out of swimsuits. Between the two rooms was a cloakroom-cum-corridor. The boys didn't realise it, but two older girls had crept over to watch them change.

I didn't get to look. Not from want of trying. The older girls were tall enough to block the view, and wouldn't let anyone else near. They described what they saw (inaccurately, I later realised. For years afterwards I believed the male member had a spiralling ridge going down it, the physical equivalent of the verb 'to screw'. When someone's older sister had a boyfriend, she was 'being screwed').

Awkward Years

During the last year of school, my best friend was one of my male cousins. We had the same colouring, the same small, sharp features and freckles. People often mistook us for twins. During the summer my cousin and I were at a swimming-pool. He had been asking about some girls I knew. I was vaguely dismayed that his taste in women was running to the obvious—tall blondes and dark-haired girls with chests that everyone stares at. Our friendship was becoming uneasy. Being related we felt we could—and we did—share everything. And because of our age, attraction was possible—but, obviously, off-limits. When the subject of sex came up, being shy and clever we couched it in the most neutral terms possible. 'If I wasn't your cousin and didn't know you, I'd probably be attracted to you.'

'Me too. If I wasn't your cousin. And didn't know you.' And we knew what we meant. Then an awkward silence, followed by a simulated farting noise, brought things back to the mundane. These conversations foretold the sort of relationships I would have with men through university: a parade of pale, gentle boys who were too shy to admit their desire until they were too drunk to care.

I pulled myself up the side of the pool and scrambled out in the direction of our towels, grabbed them both, walked back to the water.

'Hey,' he said, a little louder than was absolutely necessary. 'You're walking differently. Does that mean you're not a virgin anymore?'

'Yeah,' I said, straight-faced. He started to get out of the pool, and I threw his towel in the water. When his mum came to collect us we both sat in the back of the car, and he whispered names.

'Marc?'

'No.' Marc was in my year at school and taller than the other boys. He tended to spit when he spoke, and followed me around too often.

'Justin?'

'No.' I had a crush on Justin. Before leaving for university I told him in a letter; he never spoke to me again.

'Eric. Has to be.'

The joke candidate. 'No way!' I yelped, but refrained from giving him a nipple-twister, because that would have compromised the air of maturity the entire lie had conferred.

Within a month it happened for real, with my cousin's best friend. I flinched but didn't make a noise. And as far as I can tell, my gait was no different the day after from how it was the day before.

Exchanging Sex for Money

The day after my first client was like that. I woke up at home and held my hand up, stared at it for ages. Was something supposed to be different? Should I have felt victimised, abused? I couldn't say. The finer points of feminist theory didn't seem to apply. Things felt as they always had. Same hand, same girl. I got up and made breakfast.

By 1992 I had been studying French for six years. There, was a Canadian girl at school, Françoise, who told me that [French author] Marguerite Duras was 'sexy'. So I bought a copy of the shortest of her books I could find, because my French wasn't really very good. The book was *L'amant*. I didn't like it. For a dozen or more pages she writes about the heat in Asia, a silk dress, a hat. She describes a girl like me—small for her age, burdened with a heavy mass of hair, delicate and odd. Françoise must have been lying. But Duras's art snuck up on me and by the last page I was in tears. Something that did not happen to me broke my heart. I grew angry with myself for being so sentimental.

Actually, I am awfully sentimental. It's easy to block out the people at work; eventually their names and desires become a faceless mass of flesh if I don't write it down. But I miss being in a relationship, miss holding someone all night for the sake of breathing in tandem. Little things—the pillow my last boyfriend used, the way it smells—those stay firmly lodged in the hindbrain, ready to rear up unexpectedly.

Most of the women I've met in this field are single. A few are not. I wasn't when I started. The manager of the agency is seeing someone, but he doesn't know what she does. I'm not certain I could lie that well. How does she explain her two mobiles? When I started escorting, my then-boyfriend was present at the photo session for the agency portfolio. We split not long after. The Boy always said it didn't bother him but I'm not sure. Our last and most bitter arguments were about money, not my job. But there would have been no arguments were I not making more in two hours than he made each week. I've been on dates since then, usually with friends of friends. But it's difficult to make a connection when you're in it for the emotion and not the sex. I get enough sex on the job and on my own. I won't waste my time on anything less than partner material, not right now. And I miss the Boy—it will take an extraordinary person to match the way I felt in his arms.

The family aren't quite aware of what I do. Or if they are, they keep shtum about it. They know I work in a sex-related industry and probably tell their friends I'm in marketing at Myla. We've always been close. They know I support legalising brothels, hard drugs and other socially awkward habits. If the crime and disease surrounding these activities can be reduced through legalisation and protection, and if the government can collect tax from it, what is the problem? It all makes for interesting, if perhaps not child-friendly, discussion over supper.

My closest friends know. These are people I've trusted with far more important knowledge and who knew me when. What are friends if they don't know enough to destroy you? Some of them know other women who have been call-girls. London has an extraordinary number of escorts. I receive e-mails almost daily from people who have been in the business or dated someone who was, and each one confounds even my expectations—here are interesting, well-spoken people for whom the explicit commodification of sex is preferable to the hawthorn thicket of modern relationships.

A Sex Worker as a Confessional Writer

The job isn't always fun; no work is. There are clients I don't particularly like, though so far none I've had difficulties with. They are paying for a fantasy, so my own problems and desires are put to the side. It's about customer service. We girls sometimes have a giggle about them later on, but they are largely very nice, very lonely people. The city is an isolating place. Personal connections are hard to make.

Is it what the Little Alice imagined she'd be when she grew up? No. My dreams for the future revolved more around how I felt than what I would be doing. And this lark, writing about sex, isn't the fulfilment of a long-term goal. When I started my weblog it wasn't to crowbar my way into the literati. I found my situation mildly funny and perhaps interesting for others to read about.

I began to write anonymously for several reasons. I don't plan to stay in this field forever; some day I want to have a real job in the subject I studied. Also, it is easier to write frankly under a pseudonym. People still do not think that women can have sexual lives and yet be respected for their character and intelligence. This is not true for men. Plus I didn't want to get escorting work from men hoping to see themselves in print. And I didn't want to compromise client confidentiality.

I plan to remain anonymous for several reasons. It would embarrass my friends and family; they don't deserve that. I can take any slings and arrows the press choose to throw but would feel terrible if I put my loved ones through all this. In any case, my manager's job is illegal, and I suspect she would be in a world of trouble.

Some people accuse me of being fake, and I'm flattered that anyone thinks my writing so good that I could not be real. Unfortunately for the conspiracy theorists, there is no conspiracy. I am a young woman, I have sex for money, and I love to read and write. My taste in books shouldn't come as a surprise. After all, this job affords more spare time than most. Think of Occam's razor, the principle of parsimony: what would be simpler—that I am who I say I am, and write about, or that I am a famous author living a double life, unable to tell anyone and having a joke at the expense of my agent, publisher and readers?

What does bother me is the presumption that a person's occupation is a reflection of their intelligence or value to society: I have known plumbers who were geniuses and surgeons who couldn't tie their own shoelaces. But there are thousands of wittier, sharper authors in the world. I'd sooner spend my future as a reader than a writer.

Interview with a Male Sex Worker

Cindy-Lou Dale

Sven works as a male prostitute with both male and female clients. He resents the fact that social critics suggest that prostitutes are "selling themselves," when he is in fact being paid for a service. He considers himself morally neutral about prostitution; since he only has sex with consenting adults, no one is being coerced. Some of his clients are married, but he believes that sex outside of married relationships provides a needed outlet. He is also critical of religion for confining sex to within marriage, a mandate that eliminates sexual contact for anyone incapable of entering into a marital commitment. In the beginning, Sven disliked being a prostitute, and he used drugs to help him cope with his situation. Later, however, he developed a more positive attitude and no longer needed drugs.

"Why are male sex workers largely being ignored by the media?" I asked.

"Maybe because most of the people in the media make use of our services," he smiled.

"But the television media, producers, politicians—they're all alike," Sven continued. "Following their purported studies, they produce documentaries that only serve to make the fat cats fatter and assist politicians in keeping the masses in place. What benefit has prostitution or the escort industry derived from these television shows? We're just considered another group of misfits to look down upon by those in society that are insecure and emotionally impaired."

"Tell me about your work and ethics," I asked.

Cindy-Lou Dale, "London: Interview with a Male Sex Worker," *The Travel Diva*, August 3, 2007. www.gonomad.com/traveldiva/2007/08/london-interview-with-malesex-worker.html. Reproduced by permission.

"I get a little peeved when I hear people referring to escorts as *selling themselves*. The only way I could sell myself would be into slavery. I'm not a commodity. I provide a service by offering my companionship, and sexual skills. As you use your skill to transcribe this interview into an article I use my body as the vehicle for delivering my service. I charge £350 to act as an event escort and £750 for the full house."

"I'm morally neutral about being a male sex worker. It's how I'm used that gives it moral value. Paying for sex presents no ethical meaning. It's not good nor is it bad, it's merely a deed. My boundary is that I only have sex with a consenting adult. Be they male or female."

"How do you cope with this lifestyle," I asked.

"I've been doing this for so long now there is nothing to cope with. This is my life. In the beginning it was rough and I spiked—I needed to do drugs to try and forget but then I got over it. I realized it wasn't my soul I was selling, just a service. Everything started to go smoothly from that point and I stopped taking drugs."

Moral and Religious Concerns

We spoke of his clientele and I enquired about his ethics when called upon by heterosexual males he knows to be in a relationship.

"Most of the people that make use of my services are married or attached men. Some are heterosexual and a few are homosexual. Some want excitement, while others need a secret escape from outside their bonds. Some are straight first timers wanting to release their sexual fantasies. But regardless of what you may think, these acts do not threaten their private relationship. I think it supports it."

"What about morals?" I enquired.

"I cannot dictate the morals of the next man—that's a personal thing and the client needs to deal with that. Sometimes it's more about balancing their sexuality, as all they need is to be intimate with another man as a therapy, without necessarily having a gay lifestyle.

"I do not rape or seduce my clients; they find me through my adverts or via the internet. We speak on the phone and set up a mutually convenient date. It's all very civilized. I don't chase after them or hang about in bars, hoping to turn a few tricks. I don't get young straight guys drunk and then lead them into sin; on the contrary I'm a professional businessman." ...

We spoke of religion and Sven made a few poignant observations about extremists' opinions of sex workers.

"Imagine how much more screwed up society would be if we all followed the doctrine whereby sex is only permissible within the confines of marriage. What of those people who are incapable of having such a relationship due to their personal circumstances? Would it be more acceptable for that person to exploit or hurt another when craving closeness and take them by force? Where are the morals in that? Surely it makes sense to go to a professional?"

Confessions of an Ivy League Call Girl

Jeannette Angell

Angell believes that her profession—working as an "Ivy League lady of pleasure"—makes people nervous because she seems no different than someone's mother, daughter, or sister. She began working as a call girl because she needed money, and she adjusted to her new job easily. Although she met at least one violent client, most of the men were fairly ordinary; many were lonely and socially awkward, and the social aspect of the relationship sometimes proved more important to the client than sex. Angell eventually left the profession and recorded her memoirs in Callgirl: Confessions of an Ivy League Lady of Pleasure. *She likes to remind people that they should be careful when they judge women who work as prostitutes: these women could be their mothers, sisters, or daughters.*

People ask so many questions about it. You did that? You're kidding, right? What's it really like? What kinds of people use the service? What kinds of girls work for it? Men, especially, are utterly fascinated by the subject. It's like getting a glimpse into some mysterious semi-forbidden world, a world caricatured by pornography and attacked by conservatives and speculated about by just about everybody. Men get a vicarious sexual frisson thinking about it. Women wonder what it would be like to have someone pay—and pay well—for something they routinely give away. And, inescapably, people look at me and get a little scared. I could be—I am—one of them. I am their sister, their neighbor, their girlfriend. I'm nobody's idea of what a whore looks like. Maybe that's why I'm scary.

They want callgirls to be different, identifiable. That keeps them safe. The reality, of course, is that usually we're not. Oh,

Jeannette Angell, "Confessions of an Ivy League Call Girl," *Callgirl*, Permanent Press, Sag Harbor, NY: 2004. © 2004 by Jeannette L. Angell. All rights reserved. Reproduced by permission.

the girls on the streets at night, yeah, with them, you know. But callgirls—women who work for escort services, especially expensive ones, especially those run by other women—we don't look any different than anyone else. Not even always prettier. So we're scary. Because, you know, we could be you, too.

Maybe we are.

A Profession that Pays Well

I had a master's from Yale and had just received my doctorate in social anthropology. I was anticipating tenure-track employment. What I got instead was a series of lecturer positions, because most universities were no longer offering professorships or offering very few. I was teaching on a semester-by-semester basis, being paid the less-than-princely sum (before taxes) of $1,300 per class. And I needed money. I needed a lot of money, and I needed it quickly. I needed the money because Peter, my most recent boyfriend, had not only decided to fly to San Francisco to meet up with some ex, but had emptied my checking account before leaving. A prince among men. Rent was due. The decimated bank account had held all the money I had to live on until the end of the semester.

So I picked up the *Phoenix*, and I opened the "After Dark" section and read the ads. I circled one.

The woman on the other end of the line, who I will call Peach, ran an agency that could be considered a midlevel escort service. How can I explain it? She didn't get the rock stars when they came to town, but she did get their entourages. She got people who owned companies, but not necessarily companies anyone had ever heard of.

Peach's employees stood out in that she required a minimum of some college education. The fact is that she helped pay off a whole lot of graduate student loans. She had a specialty niche: She did well with clients who wanted intelligent conversation along with their sex.

Her clients were university faculty, stockbrokers, and lawyers. They were computer geeks who couldn't tell a C-cup from a C-drive. They owned restaurants, nightclubs, and health spas. They were handicapped, busy, socially inept, about to be married. They saw girls in offices, restaurants, boats, their own marriage beds, seedy motels, strip malls, and suites at the Park Plaza. They were the most invisible, unremarkable group of men in Boston, having in common only that they could afford to spend $200 for an hour of company.

The Call Girl as Consultant

They used the time in a variety of ways and that is my usual response when someone—and someone will, inevitably, in any conversation about the profession—says something judgmental about the perceived degradation of exchanging sex for money. Because, in my experience, that doesn't make sense. You think I'm just manipulating semantics here, don't you? I'm not: Hear me out. Many people are paid by the hour, right? An employer hires a consultant, for example, on the basis of certain areas of expertise the consultant can offer. The employer—or client—pays for the consultant's time by the hour. A callgirl is a consultant, using her expertise and experience in seduction and giving pleasure to fulfill a verbal contract with a client who is paying her by the hour. She is a skilled professional possessing knowledge for which there is a demand and for which the client is willing to pay her a predetermined rate.

If there's such a gulf between these two people, if there is more degradation in one than in the other, I'd like you to explain it to me. I have women friends who are waitresses in so-called sophisticated restaurants on Newbury Street, and I'm sorry, but I would never put up with what they have to endure every night. Not for any amount of money.

Speaking of the money, it's a pretty good hourly rate. Remember that what we get, we don't have to share with anybody—no state or federal tax, no social security. I take that back: it's a damned good hourly rate.

Occasionally there is no sex. Lonely men sometimes are just looking for company, for someone to listen to them: That's worth the fee. I remember a scene in *Frankie and Johnny*, when Al Pacino, newly released from prison, hires a woman to "spoon" with him—allow him to fall asleep curled into the curve of her body, her arms around him. I always found that scene incredibly touching.

The reality, however, is that most clients do want sex. Some want it quickly and efficiently, after which the girl is free to go; others want it as part of a date-like interlude. And there's every imaginable situation in between.

First Night on the Job

Peach was brisk on the phone. "You can refuse any call if you don't like the sound of the guy, or how it feels," she said. "You can say no to anything you don't want to do, and I'll back you up." I could have sworn I heard her stifle a yawn. I was far from yawning, myself. I answered with trepidation, but apparently I gave the right answers. Evidently, I passed the test to which I was being subjected. There was the briefest of pauses. "Hmm. All right. I'll have you see Bruce tonight. He'll like you."

"Tonight?" For all my eagerness, that seemed very soon. Panic set in. "Peach, I'm not dressed." I was wearing jeans and a T-shirt with a black vest and an olive linen jacket. Not my image of how a callgirl should dress. (Like I knew anything: I had seen *Half Moon Street* and *Pretty Woman*. What you might call a limited frame of reference.)

Peach was dismissive. "Don't worry—you're dressed perfectly. A lot of the clients go for casual. So do it, or not. Call me at 7, if you want, and I'll set it up."

And that was that. Do it, or not.

I decided to do it.

Bruce seemed pleasant enough on the phone (I had been expecting a stutterer, maybe?) and gave me directions to a local marina. He lived, it transpired, on a boat.

He was a bear of a man, bearded, with eyes that twinkled behind his glasses. We sat on a sofa in the cabin of his sailboat, drank a very nice chilled Montrachet, and talked about music, our conversation interspersed with clumsy silences. It felt oddly familiar. To tell you the truth, what it felt like was a date. A first date.

He went to refill our glasses, and when he came back, he did the classic yawn and stretch—the favorite move from everybody's first junior-high romance. But at that moment, I leaned forward to pick up my glass, so he missed. Finally, he kissed me. A first date kiss.

It was at that precise moment that I knew it was going to be all right. This wasn't anything esoteric or bizarre or dangerous: this was something I had done before, something I did well, and—best of all—something I enjoyed doing.

Later, I learned that some callgirls won't kiss, that they consider their lips the only part of themselves they can withhold. I disagree. Maybe the pretense of romance is better than no romance at all. Or maybe I just like to kiss.

Can I tell you this? It was better sex than I'd had with the rat bastard boyfriend. Ever. And I was getting paid for it. I felt like singing, or skipping, something joyous and happy. I had just spent a pleasant evening. After I took out the $60 that was Peach's fee, I had made $140. In one hour. Anybody else out there making that kind of money?

Ordinary Johns

There was a guy up in North Andover, a handsome, middle-aged black man who I saw from time to time. After a semi-successful three quarters of an hour on his bed, he would make out a check (previously cleared with Peach, of course; this tends to be a cash-only business), always with a flourish. He winked at me as he wrote that it was for the "purchase of artwork." There was a ridiculously young man in South Boston, nice, who offered me a light beer and never gave me a chance to drink it. There was my first hotel client, a regular who visited once a month on business. He was very busy, he informed me, gesturing toward his open laptop on the coffee table. He was as good as his word. I was out of there in under 20 minutes. It was 8:30 at night, and I was walking down a hotel corridor with $150 that I had made in less time than it had taken me to get dressed.

None of these men had a particularly scintillating personality. One kept following up his remarks with, "Oh, you probably don't understand that. Like, who am I talking to here, Einstein or something?" "True," I agreed, the third time he said it. "Einstein's doctorate wasn't in anthropology, mine is." He was pretty much quiet after that.

All in all, they weren't bad people. Ordinary, marginally attractive, with questionable social skills, yes. Dull, predictable, full of insecurities, sure. I had dated men just like them in the past and for no compensation.

Among my regulars there was Phil, who liked to show me off to his friends. We sipped cocktails together in trendy restaurants on Columbus Avenue, chatting with all the people he knew who "accidentally" happened by that night, before going back to his place for sex.

Robert took me to wine-tasting parties at Cornucopia on the Wharf. We'd sit at big circular tables and listen to the distributors discuss the wines while we ate and sipped, and he watched the other man watching my breasts.

For Raoul, I dressed in little black nothing cocktail dresses and went to the symphony and the occasional opera. We ate dinner first, wonderful dinners. The sex always seemed to be an afterthought. More frequently than not he would ask if I'd terribly mind skipping that final portion of the evening; he was in his sixties, and quite naturally got tired. I always managed to express regret.

You walk along Commonwealth Avenue down near the Public Garden and Beacon Street with its wrought-iron fences, and you wonder about who lives behind the mullioned windows and thick velvet draperies. You imagine that they must be people of culture. So when Peach sent me to Beacon Street, I felt nothing but a sense of mild anticipation.

Sleeping with the Enemy

Her directions led me to a fourth-floor apartment that overlooked the Charles, and as soon as I got there, moved toward the window with an exclamation of delight. But this client—Barry by name—wasn't paying me to enjoy the view. I know this to be true because he said so, even as he grasped my arm and pulled me away from the window, a grasp that was to leave clear, deep imprints of his fingers on my bruised skin.

Barry pinned me against a brick wall, and it hurt. His hands hurt, too, pushing against me, squeezing my breasts. I gasped and pulled away and told him to stop. He laughed. He actually laughed. "You don't tell me to do anything," he said. "You're just a whore. You do what I say."

I remember being pushed onto the bed, with him on top of me. I remember his voice, over and over. "You're just a whore, aren't you? You're just a dirty little whore. Say it! Say you're a whore!" I struggled away and crouched next to the headboard. No amount of money was worth this. I took a deep breath and screamed. And did it again.

Barry sat on the bed, the fury draining from him. He stalked toward the bathroom. "Don't slam the door on your way out," he said, coldly. "I'm taking a shower. You made me feel dirty."

I had made him feel dirty.

Later, I met a woman named Margot who also worked for the agency. Over drinks at Jillian's, we began sharing client experiences. Barry, it turned out, was one of Margot's regulars. I stared at her. "How can you stand him?"

"Well, see, I have this theory." Margot took a liberal swallow of her Manhattan. "Guys like Barry, they have so much rage against women, you know?" "No shit," I muttered.

"Okay. So he keeps pacing around his apartment and muttering about women being whores. Maybe he watches them through his windows, pretty women down on the Esplanade or Memorial Drive, and it's stoking his feelings of insecurity and inadequacy—well, eventually there will be too much pressure, and it'll blow." She sipped her drink before delivering the punch line. "So if the pressure gets eased, maybe he won't blow. Maybe if he can play out his sick little fantasy with one of us from time to time, with someone who can handle it, you know, then he won't walk down Beacon Street one night and follow some innocent woman home. Maybe he won't hurt her."

I liked Margot's theory. Everything I'd been reading about prostitution was about how it contributed to the oppression of women, how it perpetuated men's fantasies of control and power. And here was this woman, calmly sipping her Manhattan and telling me she was considering the needs of other women. I liked the thought of that anonymous woman walking down Beacon Street at night, her footsteps echoing. I liked thinking that she was safe because somewhere four stories up, Margot was there, sleeping with the enemy.

Leaving the Business Behind

I don't know, in the end, why I left. I'm not even sure it matters. Take your pick: I left because I got scared, or because I got hurt, or because I grew up, grew out of it.

In the end, I think that I left because it was simply time to leave.

The business had given me what I needed. It gave me financial security. And maybe, too, it gave me the thrill of having lived on the edge for a while.

Sometimes, even now, when it's around 7 o'clock, I'll stop and wonder what's going on tonight. Who's working, what clients will call, that sort of thing. It won't be anybody that I know, not anymore. Time has moved on, in this business faster than anywhere else.

But the names don't matter. The needs will always be the same. Telephones will ring; girls will fix their makeup in vanity mirrors. Tonight, as every night, money will change hands. Callgirls will give pleasure, excitement, mystery, hope, enchantment.

I stop and I think. Then I shrug and head out to the bike path for a ride, or I load the kids into the car.

I have told one story—mine. I willingly and deliberately entered the employment of an escort agency. I do not regret having made that decision.

Because agencies like Peach's exist, agencies that do not exploit or injure their employees, a number of women like myself were and continue to be able to attain a measure of financial security in a society where it is difficult for a woman to do so. I am aware, however, and most urgently want you to be aware, that many women are not in this profession because they need to pay off student loans. I have a positive story to tell. I'm not at all sure that my experience is that of most women involved in this business.

Please don't be so quick to call us hookers, to judge us. We could be your mother, your sister, your girlfriend, your daughter. Even your college professor.

No, I take that back. It's not a matter of saying that we could be. We are.

SOCIAL ISSUES
FIRSTHAND

CHAPTER 2

The Ethics and Politics of Prostitution

The Unionization of Sex Workers

Ana Lopez, as told to Workers Solidarity Movement

While simultaneously attending graduate school and working in the sex industry, Ana Lopez decided to conduct her PhD research on sex workers. After speaking with a number of people, however, she realized that she needed to take her research a step further and form a union. During interviews, she had discovered that many people who worked in the sex industry lacked the same labor rights that many people in other professions took for granted. The International Union of Sex Workers (IUSW) would fulfill this need, advocating for prostitutes, dancers, and others in the sex industry. Because many sex workers operate in an underground economy, basic issues like safety have seldom been addressed. In order to attend to these needs, the IUSW has worked to decriminalize prostitution, a change that would allow governments to protect instead of prosecute sex workers. The IUSW also works to improve the image of sex workers, arguing that choosing to work within the sex industry is no more undignified than working at McDonald's.

Workers Solidarity Movement: Can you please introduce yourself and the union you are part of and helped start.

Ana Lopez: My name is Ana Lopez from the International Union of Sex Workers (IUSW). I was one of the founders of IUSW. I was working as a sex worker in London when I finished my masters and wanted to start a PhD. Since I was working in this area, I decided that I would do research for my PhD within the sex industry. I don't believe in science for science sake, I believe that any kind of research should be en-

Workers Solidarity Movement, "Interview with Ana Lopez from the International Union of Sex Workers," *Red & Black Revolution*, Spring 2007. www.wsm.ie. Reproduced by permission.

gaged and useful for the people you have studied. I started doing what we call strategic research, where you ask the people you want to study what they think is an interesting topic or area that needs to be studied and what kind of information they need to gather to respond to those needs.

I did my pilot interview with people from different sectors of the sex industry: from prostitution, street workers, pornography models and actors. And I asked them these kinds of questions. What I found out from this initial group of people was that one of the main complaints was that they felt very isolated and they didn't have a collective voice. They were telling me they needed a collective voice in order to eliminate the exploitation that they faced. This group of people didn't feel that their work was inherently bad or immoral in any sense, but they felt that they were forced to work in exploitative conditions because of the legislation and because of the stigma attached to their work. They also wanted to respond to the way the media portrayed them. The general public only has the media to understand what sex work is all about and they show a very black and white picture that doesn't do justice to the realities and multiple experiences within sex work.

When I heard all of this I interpreted it from my activist background that they weren't giving me a topic of research but a call for action. And I thought that I had the responsibility to have this action happen with their help. So I called my pilot interviewees for a meeting in my flat over tea and cookies and we talked about this kind of research. I asked them if they were really serious about this and if they would like to create this type of platform and collective in which we can demand our rights.

When it was clear that this was what people wanted, we then defined our mission statement and what we were there for. We decided that we were there to fight for rights for all types of sex workers, especially labour rights. We felt that what was wrong with the way people saw sex workers till then was that it was discussed within the realm of feminism, gender and morality. What we were saying was that it was work, and the reason all of us are in this industry is that we need to pay our bills at the end of each month. So if we treat it as any other work, as a labour issue, then we can find solutions. And solutions are to be found in eliminating the exploitative conditions and not eliminating the industry altogether. . . . What you do in other exploitative industries also applies here. Women and transgender people get exploited in many other industries unfortunately. But the response of the feminist and trade union movement in relation to those other industries is to eliminate the exploitation and not the industry itself. We wanted to get in line with all other workers. Basically that's how it got started.

How have you gone about getting members into the union, outside of your personal network?

At the beginning we started by publishing a magazine, we called it *RESPECT!* (Rights and Equality for Sex Professionals and Employees in Connected Trades). This magazine has articles written about sex work and by sex workers. We were able to go to different places where sex workers operate, we had something to offer and something to talk about. We also set up a web site and a discussion list. These two things were instrumental in making this group international. When we started we called ourselves international, but we started as a small group based in London so we were not international. Through the web site people have joined from all over the world, we have more than 2000 members on the discussion list.

Would you have members from all different aspects of sex work?

The two most dominant groups are people who work in prostitution (I mean all types of prostitution; people who work on the streets, people who work indoors, people who work in S&M, escorts) and people who work in dance—strip tease, pole dancing etc. Those are the biggest groups, but we also have models, actresses and phone sex operators.

In terms of the work that is legal at the moment, what are the rights you are fighting for?

The right to have a proper contract, having a proper code of conduct in the place you work so it is clear what you are allowed and not allowed to do, for the managers and clients to know what they are allowed and not allowed to do. It is important that these are written down and made very clear, and if someone breaks those rules there must be mechanisms to address that and penalise the one who broke the rules. So it's very important to have grievance procedures like most other work places. Now there are a couple of clubs that are unionised and you can find these things.

Also Health and Safety rights, something that is basic in most other work places that is ignored in the sex industry. People are using their bodies in their work, they are dancing and wearing high heels. For instance, you can't expect dancers who are wearing high heels to be going up and down stairs, it is not safe at all. You cannot expect them to dance doing floor work if the floor is not clean. And you can't use abrasive cleaning products to clean poles because people are going to use those poles to lean against.

How about the illegal aspects of sex work, what is the union trying to fight for there?

We are calling for the decriminalisation of sex work, prostitution specifically, since all the establishments in that area are illegal. Prostitution itself is legal but everything around it is illegal. There is hardly any way you can do this as a profession . . . without breaking the law somehow. That is what makes it such a dangerous and underground activity. We are using the political clout of the union to put pressure on governments to decriminalise prostitution.

Would the goal be to eliminate street prostitution and have safe legal indoor spaces?

No, that is something that the general public thinks would be a good idea, and unfortunately politicians as well, but that wouldn't be a fair type of situation. That kind of idea comes from people thinking that no one would work on the streets if they had the choice. That's not true, many people would prefer to work on the streets because there is freedom attached to that; you are independent, you don't have a boss, you decide what type of hours you want to work. For many people that is very important. What we would call for is legal establishments so that people can work in those establishments legally. In that situation you would have less people working on the streets. And for those who choose to work on the streets, the idea is that they can work in safety, in safety zones. It might not be the ideal but there are examples where it is working really well in the Netherlands and in Edinburgh, so that is the model we have been pointing to. These areas are appointed by the local authorities as areas that prostitution takes place in and police will be there to protect the sex workers rather than arrest them. These areas would be well lit so there are less chances of being attacked by potentially dangerous or violent clients.

On your web site you say that the percentage of women who experience trafficking is quite low, yet in the media it would seem that this is a huge problem; can you speak about that?

This is an industry where lots and lots of people want to migrate. Sex workers are often the most entrepreneurial people within their company. In this industry there is always a need for new faces, so to be a successful sex worker you have to move from one place to another. If you want to earn money you are going to move to another country where someone told you where you can make more money. People often just want to move for the sake of moving.

So there is a lot of migration, very often people do not have the opportunity to migrate in a legal way so they will need a third party helping them in this process of migration.

Because it is an illegal industry, an illegal process of migration, this leaves many opportunities for these third parties to exploit sex workers. In migration it's a process you can compare to a lottery; some people are very lucky and they make a lot of money in the country they migrated to. Some people have very bad stories to tell. There is a continuum of situations. In one extreme you have people who have been successful and in the other extreme you have people who have experienced exploitative situations, such as slavery. We cannot let this happen, even if it's one person it's not acceptable. There is a sense that the media makes this into hype, a moral fear. You would have the impression that all migration is trafficking and it's not. Those situations with exploitation and where people have no freedom of movement are in a tiny minority if you compare it to the phenomenon that is migration. To look at this you have to look at migration first. . . .

In debunking myths about prostitution and showing the positive role prostitutes have in society, you talk about the prostitute's role with people with physical and other disabilities that for whatever reason can't masturbate themselves and/or are unable to have sexual relationships with other people. It would seem that that aspect of sex worker's clientele would be quite small and it would be more the rich white businessmen who are using the service and maintaining the power and hierarchical dynamics in the rest of the society. Can you speak on this?

Possibly they are not such a small minority as you imagine. I know many sex workers that make most of their money with the city workers and businessmen so they can have time to dedicate to clients who have disabilities so they don't need to charge as much. These are areas that are growing.

There is a demand for whatever reason for sexual services. I believe the market is growing because until recently the only people who had economic power to use sexual services were businessmen, male, with high economic status. I think things are changing and more and more women have economic power to access sexual services. There is still a lot of stigma attached to that. I think when women are accessing sex workers it's through the internet so they are not seen as using these services.

I don't see much of a division between the entertainment industry and the sex industry. In my grandmother's time if you chose to be a theatre actress it was as good as being a sex worker. You would be labelled as a whore and a slut and you wouldn't have a high status in society at all. And this has changed tremendously, now singers and actresses have very high status.

It seems like prostitution is not like every other type of work. It is many women's experience to be treated like they are prostitutes, that they get treated as an object to be used and that they are expected to use their body to repay a favour that a male has done for them. And women get treated like prostitutes every day without having made the choice to go into that profession.

Thank you for asking this question, it is one that no [one] has asked me in a long time and it is the reason for my activism. No woman is free till all sex workers are free. It is exactly that stigma, that we can call the whore stigma, that is not limited to sex workers. We sex workers feel that every woman on the planet at a certain point feels that stigma, since it is attached to all women. So that's why I think that all women should join in solidarity to fight for our rights. Because at any point you can be called a whore, if there is no reason for that to be a stigma then we all can be free. That will stop being an insult when sex workers are treated with dignity like any other worker and when no sex worker is in this industry against their will. And that is the role of the union and sex worker self organisation, to make sure that no one is in this industry against their will and those that are in the industry can work with full labour rights with dignity and respect. I think sex workers organising should be inspiring for other workers. Because we work with our bodies it is obvious that no one should control our bodies, and that we should be able to do whatever we want with our own bodies.

And if we manage to organise and do our work on our own terms, and have control of our industry in the least organised and the most marginalised of workers, then any worker can do that, and I hope this inspires other workers to see that no one should have control over their body and their work. They should control their own industries. When people realise that, then we can get rid of capitalism and have global revolution.

You mentioned in your talk that the people that were part of your pilot interview all made an informed decision to work in the sex industry, do you think this represents the wider community?

They were a network of friends, many of whom were involved in other forms of activism as well, so I would not generalise this across all those in the industry. Yet I can say after five years of activism and working in the industry and so on that that is a great majority. It is only a small minority that doesn't make an informed decision to enter this industry.

From many women I know, they have said they consider going into sex work at some level, let it be phone work and so on, due to feeling extreme poverty. And other women have said that in the back of their minds they knew it was always an option because they were a woman. I would not consider these situations to be informed decisions, but rather desperation.

Yet that applies to any other industry. I wouldn't consider working in McDonald's because at this time I'm not desperate. Let's say this year or the year after I'm really desperate for money, maybe I would work at McDonald's or clean toilets, things that I would never imagine myself doing. Things that I think are more undignified and humiliating than working in the sex industry. People have different images of what they want to do, and different ideas of what is humiliating and what is an ok type of work. I think that poverty is not enough to explain sex work because on one hand you have people in poverty who do not work in the sex industry, who choose to do other things, and many people who do work in the sex industry who are not in poverty and have many other possibilities. I know many people in the industry who have degrees, who have left other careers to work in the sex industry and so on. What you cannot do is generalise in this industry, you have multiple realities. People come from different situations and social and economic backgrounds.

You mentioned that part of your struggle is fighting capitalism and I was wondering if in your ideal society capitalism didn't exist and society was self organised, do you think sex work would exist and if so how would it be organised?

I think that in my ideal utopian society people would not have sex for money, but people would not do teaching for money, they would do everything for love because they wanted to. That is what I'm working for. While we have to live under capitalism, I think it's really unfair to pick on sex workers. We are all selling ourselves, we are all selling our labour under capitalism. So don't pick on sex workers and expect sex workers to do something different from what everyone else is doing.

I think there is a revolutionary potential among sex workers because they are the most oppressed and marginalised of workers, and if this group is able to stand up for their rights and take control of the huge industry it would be an inspiration for all. Because it's underground there is lots of corruption; if we can manage to take control, then any worker can do that.

You were asking me a question of sex work being like any type of work and I didn't really address that. I think sex work is a specific type of work, in a sense it is not like any other type of work. There are many other industries that you are using your own body and that doesn't mean you shouldn't have the full range of labour and human rights and that you shouldn't be respected, I'm thinking about an industry that is marginal to the sex industry and that is the fashion industry. A few years ago when Miss World was held in London, we went to the place where the competition was taking place with banners and leaflets inviting the contestants to join the union, because they also are working with their bodies. They are also working in a corrupt industry. But they have rights, not full rights—that's why we are asking them to join the union. They are still very much exploited, they can make lots of money but the ones organising the fashion industry are making much more money. And they experience many of the same problems such as being pushed onto drugs and such things. My point is that they have a different status in society, they are viewed as successful women, young women strive to be like them, and they are all over mainstream magazines. So I ask what is the difference, why can they enjoy respect and a positive view from society and sex workers can't.

When you do sex work you are in danger of getting very emotionally involved, clients are very close to you, your body and so on. There are many professions where this happens. I think if I was a psychiatrist for instance I would not be able to deal with people's emotional problems and switch off at five o'clock in the evening. Yes you have to learn to deal with all this emotional baggage that comes with it.

The other thing that is interesting was that I had to tell my mother my work. My mother for many years was a child minder, that was commodification of child care, which in our society is viewed as even more sacred than sex—the mother's love is something that is very sacred. Under capitalism even that is made into a commodity. My mother used to organise five of these women doing this work, their work was to take care of other children for the day and at the end of the day they go home. And I told my mother you are the equivalent of a brothel mother, you are organising groups of women to do something that in our ideal society would be done for love and not for money. And it is also something that triggers a basic instinct, of motherly love. So these women would love these children for money for a few hours, and then these children would disappear. The biggest difference between my mother and the women that work for her is that they are legal, they are actually seen as doing something good in society's eyes and they have rights and a sex worker doesn't.

In supporting this kind of initiative of sex workers organizing, you don't necessarily have to agree with my view that sex work is a legitimate type of work, and that it's not inherently exploitative. When we were in the union meeting there were different members from different industries, and I tried to pass a motion calling for decriminalising prostitution. Then people got to speak either for or against the motion. And one of the most interesting comments was from this [person] who worked in Sellafield [England] in the nuclear plant. He stood up and said, "I work in Sellafield and a lot of people in this room would have a serious problem with what I do and the type of things I produce. But the difference between myself and a sex worker is that I have full labour and human rights, I'm legal and I have health and safety regulations and protective equipment and so on and a sex worker does not have any of that." And I thought that was a really good argument, whatever it is you think about prostitution, whether you think it's morally wrong and so on you should still join in solidarity with this group of workers and support our fight for rights.

Sex with Prostitutes Is Exciting and Honest

Sebastian Horsley

Sebastian Horsley has spent decades visiting brothels. He has also worked as an escort and run a brothel. From his experience, he believes that anonymous sex is much more satisfying than entangled emotional commitments. A relationship ultimately feels like a trap and can only be made interesting through deception; with prostitution, one is spared the messy intimacy of love. Illegal prostitution allows a brothel creeper to add danger to his life, living—like the prostitute—outside the boundaries of the law. Many people believe that prostitution should be legalized or eradicated, but these reformers miss the point: Sex is perhaps the most natural and wholesome thing a person can pay money for, and paying for illegal sex is exciting. Prostitution may be debasing, but so are human desires. Horsley is an English writer who has penned the memoir Dandy in the Underworld, *published in September 2007.*

I remember the first time I had sex—I still have the receipt. The girl was alive, as far as I could tell, she was warm and she was better than nothing. She cost me £20.

I was 16 then and I'm 41 now. I have spent 25 years throwing my money and heart at tarts. I have slept with every nationality in every position in every country. From high-class call girls at £1,000 a pop to the meat-rack girls of Soho at £15, I have probably slept with more than 1,000 prostitutes, at a cost of £100,000.

I am a connoisseur of prostitution: I can take its bouquet, taste it, roll it around my mouth, give you the vintage. I have used brothels, saunas, private homes from the internet and or-

Sebastian Horsley, "The Brothel Creeper," *Observer*, September 19, 2004. Copyright © 2004 Guardian Newspapers Limited. Reproduced by permission of the author.

dered girls to my flat prompt as pizza. While we are on the subject, I have also run a brothel. And I have been a male escort. I wish I was more ashamed. But I'm not. I love prostitutes and everything about them. And I care about them so much I don't want them to be made legal.

In English brothels you shuffle into a seedy room so dim you can only meet the girl by Braille. But in New York last year I sat on a four-poster bed while 10 girls paraded in front of me one by one, like bowls of sushi on a carousel. 'Hi,' they would say, 'I'm Tiffany', 'I'm Harmony', 'I'm Michelle', and I would rise and kiss them. It was so touching, so sweet, so kind. There should always, no matter what, be politeness. It is the way the outside world should work, selfishly but honestly.

The great thing about sex with whores is the excitement and variety. If you say you're enjoying sex with the same person after a couple of years you're either a liar or on something. Of all the sexual perversions, monogamy is the most unnatural. Most of our affairs run the usual course. Fever. Boredom. Trapped. This explains much of the friction in our lives—love being the delusion that one woman differs from another. But with brothels there is always the exhilaration of not knowing what you're going to get.

The Advantage of Anonymous Sex

The problem with normal sex is that it leads to kissing and pretty soon you've got to talk to them. Once you know someone well the last thing you want to do is screw them. I like to give, never to receive; to have the power of the host, not the obligation of the guest. I can stop writing this and within two minutes I can be chained, in the arms of a whore. I know I am going to score and I know they don't really want me. And within 10 minutes I am back writing. What I hate are meaningless and heartless one-night stands where you tell all sorts of lies to get into bed with a woman you don't care for.

The worst things in life are free. Value seems to need a price tag. How can we respect a woman who doesn't value herself? When I was young I used to think it wasn't who you wanted to have sex with that was important, but who you were comfortable with socially and spiritually. Now I know that's rubbish. It's who you want to have sex with that's important. In the past I have deceived the women I have been with. You lie to two people in your life; your partner and the police. Everyone else gets the truth.

Part of me used to enjoy the deception. There was something about the poverty of desire with one's girlfriend. Sex without betrayal I found meaningless. Without cruelty there was no banquet. Having a secret life is exhilarating. I also have problems with unpaid-for sex. I am repulsed by the animality of the body, by its dirt and decay. The horror for me is the fact that the sublime, the beautiful and the divine are inextricable from basic animal functions. For some reason money mitigates this. Because it is anonymous.

What I hate with women generally is the intimacy, the invasion of my innermost space, the slow strangulation of my art. The writer chained for life to the routine of a wage slave and the ritual of copulation. When I love somebody, I feel sort of trapped. Three years ago I was saved. I found a girl whom I could fall in love with ... and sleep with prostitutes with. She sends me to brothels to sleep with women for her. I buy her girls for her birthday and we go to whorehouses together. I am free forever from the damp, dark prison of eternal love.

Lust over Love

A prostitute exists outside the establishment. She is either rejected by it or in opposition to it, or both. It takes courage to cross this line. She deserves our respect, not our punishment. And certainly not our pity or prayers.

Of course, the general feeling in this country is that the man is somehow exploiting the woman, but I don't believe this. In fact, the prostitute and the client, like the addict and the dealer, is the most successfully exploitative relationship of all. And the most pure. It is free of ulterior motives. There is no squalid power game. The man is not taking and the woman is not giving. . . .

Why does a sleazy bastard like me like whores so much? Why pay for it? The problem is that the modern woman is a prostitute who doesn't deliver the goods. Teasers are never pleasers; they greedily accept presents to seal a contract and then break it. At least the whore pays the flesh that's haggled for. The big difference between sex for money and sex for free is that sex for money usually costs a lot less.

But it is more than this. What I want is the sensation of sex without the boredom of its conveyance. Brothels make possible contacts of astounding physical intimacy without the intervention of personality. I love the artificial paradise; the anonymity; using money, the most impersonal instrument of intimacy to buy the most personal act of intimacy. Lust over love, sensation over security, and to fall into a woman's arms without falling into her hands.

Having an instinctive sympathy for those condemned by conventional society, I wanted to cross the line myself. To pay for sex is to strip away the veneer of artifice and civilisation and connect with the true animal nature of man. Some men proudly proclaim that they have never paid for it. Are they saying that money is more sacred than sex?

Breaking the Law for Fun

But one of the main reasons I enjoy prostitutes is because I enjoy breaking the law—another reason I don't want brothels made legal. There is a charm about the forbidden that makes it desirable. When I have dinner every evening in Soho I always think: isn't scampi delicious—what a pity it isn't illegal.

I'm sure I am not alone in this. Even Adam himself did not want the apple for the apple's sake; he wanted it only because it was forbidden.

As for the girls, the argument is that making it legal will somehow make it safer, but Soho has one of the lowest crime rates in the country. Anyway, crime and risk are part of the texture of life. Indeed, Freud tells us: 'Life loses interest when the highest stake in the game of living, life itself, may not be risked.' Risk is what separates the good part of life from the tedium.

I decided to ask my Claudia, my favourite prostitute. I first spotted her in the street in Knightsbridge 10 years ago and was so taken by her haunted beauty that I decided to follow her. There was an air of great quality about Claudia. The faces of English girls look as if there is not enough materials to go round. They have thin lips and papery eyelids, box jawbones, prominent Adam's apples and withered hearts. Claudia looks Mediterranean—her lips are full and curly, her nostrils flared, her eyes black and as big as saucers.

She walked and I stalked all the way to Soho and down Brewer Street. No. No way. She couldn't be! She turned, and walked into a brothel. I couldn't believe it. I could f--- Raquel Welch for £25.

When I ask if she wants prostitution legalised, she reacts violently: 'No way! I tried to take a regular job a few months ago. After tax and national insurance I was left with practically nothing. So I came back here. On a good day here I can take £500. I don't have a pimp, so after paying the overheads and the maid I've got more than enough.' There you are. Income tax has made more liars out of the British people than prostitution.

Prostitution as a Mirror of Man

I know a little bit about the business side. Some years ago I became a madam and a male escort. I turned one of the rooms in my flat in Shepherd Market into a knocking shop and joined an escort agency. I went into prostitution looking for love, not money. That said, I always took cash. The women wanted company, someone willing to please at the midnight hour, and straight sex. It was nerve-wracking wondering if I was going to be able to get it up or get on, but at least I had a valid reason for liking my lovers—they paid me. I didn't care if someone called me a whore and a pimp.

So you see, I have always been a prostitute by sympathy. As for the rest of society, prostitution is the mirror of man, and man has never been in danger of becoming bogged down in beauty. So why don't we leave it alone? Or learn to love it, like me? Sex is one of the most wholesome, spiritual and natural things money can buy. And like all games, it becomes more interesting when played for money. And even more so when it is illegal.

Hookers and drunks instinctively understand that common sense is the enemy of romance. Will the bureaucrats and politicians please leave us some unreality. I know what you are thinking. That it's all very well for people like me to idealise whores and thieves; to think that the street is somehow noble and picturesque; I have never had to live there. But so what? One day I will. Until such time, I have to pay for it. How else would someone young, rich and handsome get sex in this city? Yes, yes, I know. Prostitution is obscene, debasing and disgraceful. The point is, so am I.

The Uneasy Relationship Between Prostitutes and Feminists

Teri Goodson

Sex worker Teri Goodson joined the National Organization for Women (NOW) during the 1990s, believing that the organization would understand how social prejudice affects prostitutes. She soon learned, however, that many within the organization had little sympathy for sex workers. Goodson pushed for reforms within NOW, but found her struggle only partially successful. Many middle-class feminists, she states, simply fail to understand the hardships that lower-class sex workers faced. Goodson believes this situation can change if more sex workers join NOW. She asserts that feminists' disapproval of sex-worker industries only serves to reinforce society's double standard, whereby it is more acceptable for men than for women to seek erotic pleasure without emotional ties.

Women in this culture receive subtle messages from childhood onward to use their sexuality as a bargaining chip in exchange for economic security and protection from a man under the guise of "love" and family formation, but outright prostitution, while much more straightforward, is considered disreputable. This helps maintain the double standard that denies women the type of proactive freedom, pleasure, and agency accorded to men. Gender parity demands a thorough evaluation of erotic practices and politics, including an honest critique of how certain aspects of feminism reinforce rather than deconstruct the madonna/whore dichotomy.

Believing I could make a difference, I joined the San Francisco chapter of the National Organization for Women (NOW)

Teri Goodson, "A Prostitute Joins NOW," *Whores and Other Feminists* New York: Routledge, 1997, pp. 248–251. © 1997 by Routledge. All rights reserved. Republished with permission of Routledge, conveyed through Copyright Clearance Center, Inc.

in 1991. Working for over three years within NOW as an out prostitute and sex-worker advocate has been a trying but educational and rewarding experience. Originally, I had not joined with sex-worker advocacy in mind; the impetus was my outrage over Anita Hill's Senate hearing and Senator Kennedy's nephew's rape trial. The all-male Senate Hearing Committee questioned Ms. Hill's testimony with little if any sensitivity or understanding about sexual harassment. I had experienced similar unwanted advances since puberty and understood that it was an all-too-common phenomenon. During the televised Kennedy rape trial, the defense attorneys implied that the alleged victim was "asking for it," i.e., that she was a "bad" woman, a mother with her own sexual needs who dared go to bars alone to enjoy herself. These incidents lit a fire in me. I wanted women freed from the coercive social power of the sexual double standard; we couldn't allow men to retain their privileges at our expense.

When I first became a NOW member, I possessed scant knowledge about feminist sexual politics. I believed in the right to my own sexual choices without being unfairly stigmatized because my work branded me a "whore." Unaware of just how controversial commercial sex—or indeed any, "deviant" form of sexual expression, such as sadomasochism or pornography—is among feminists, I initially underestimated the commitment and resources required to educate other feminists about commercial sex and win them as allies.

NOW is a multi-issue, feminist organization whose politics are confined to gender issues affecting women; its activism does not necessarily cross over to include stigmatized forms of sexuality. Missing the overlap, NOW members often exhibit unexamined prejudices against sexual minorities common to the larger society. These prejudices can be traced to patriarchal religious and cultural traditions, rather than reason or feminism. If women refuse to question the sources of their assumptions about unconventional forms of sex, such traditions will continue to divide rather than unite women. I would like to see us create a broadly inclusive, woman-friendly sex ethos that embraces various types of erotic activities based on informed consent, mutual respect, responsibility, and the pursuit of pleasure. For many women, joyful, compassionate libertinism is a completely foreign concept. To traverse this territory, women must brave being labeled "whores"

Working Within NOW

Some non-sex-worker feminists seemed to understand that the stigma and oppression of female prostitutes is used to uphold the double standard and is limiting to all women's sexual freedom. Although NOW has been difficult to mobilize, partly because of the lack of sex-worker activists willing to work with them, I have witnessed victories, especially within San Francisco and California NOW, the two affiliates that have had the most exposure to commercial sex workers. Partly as a result of my work, during the 1994 California NOW State Conference, a resolution passed committing California NOW to work in solidarity with prostitutes' rights and advocacy groups. Prostitution bills were put on the 1995 legislation watch list, and the state PAC [Political Action Commitment] questionnaire continued asking candidates whether they favored the decriminalization of prostitution. During this time I was also able to establish a prostitution committee, an action liaison between California NOW and prostitutes' groups like COYOTE, [Call Off Your Tired Ethics].

My efforts to build bridges have not been as successful as I had hoped. It has been difficult to find like-minded activists who are willing to work within NOW. Those who try often find themselves outnumbered by their opposition, or they experience hostile attitudes from sexual conservatives who want to label us victims or patriarchal pawns. More common are apathy or ambivalence and an unwillingness to prioritize our concerns. And it's also true that many commercial sex workers are politically inexperienced; they are encouraged by society to keep their work hidden, not to discuss it publicly.

Even though National NOW passed a resolution calling for the decriminalization of prostitution in 1972, attempts at membership mobilization around this issue have failed, especially as the conservative ideological rhetoric of prostitution abolitionists and antipornography forces has gained greater acceptance. These proponents advocate eradicating prostitution, despite the effect on prostitutes' lives, and "rescuing" the women whom they often reduce to being nothing but stereotypical helpless toys for men. But if they were to learn from history and the failed social-purity campaigns during the beginning of the century, they would understand that this approach translates into worse working conditions for prostitutes, especially the more visible ones.

Feminism and Class Bias

It is presently unlikely that NOW or other women's groups will campaign for prostitution law reform without pressure from significant numbers of prostitutes. Prostitutes' work experience varies widely by socioeconomic class and other factors. Those who are better equipped to participate in political discourse by virtue of education or social status often possess the least motivation for doing so. The more successful prostitutes may or may not benefit from change, depending on the tradeoffs involved. It is very likely that, given the present conservative political climate, state intervention would create a loss of privacy, autonomy, and the higher profits a prohibited market generates. For perhaps the vast majority, the personal risks faced by publicly exposing their illegal and highly stigmatized work seem to outweigh any advantage.

Meeting other commercial sex advocates who have worked within NOW, such as Miki Demarest, Bobby Lilly, and Priscilla Alexander, helped me become more familiar with pertinent NOW history and ideology. I soon realized that if cultivation of sex-worker allies was my goal, feminist discourse about sexuality needed to be lifted onto a more sophisticated plane.

Most NOW members are not sex workers, so they may easily dismiss sex-worker issues as being "merely about sex" when seemingly more pressing matters are at hand. Yet the connection between sex and economics is an important one for all women, not just sex workers, and should not be ignored. NOW strives toward a consensus about sexuality in general while marginalizing divisive issues like commercial sex, the inclusion of which would help highlight related and equally challenging economic issues. Socioeconomic class bias often becomes evident in feminist censure of commercial sex, and some women seem unaware of their own biases. Judgmental attitudes, particularly from middle- and upper-class women, usually trigger resentment from sex workers, many of whom are working-class or poor women trying to earn a living the best way they know how. They have already been stigmatized and/or criminalized as outcasts from society and wonder why feminists would add to these woes. Is it because sex workers expose public hypocrisy, myths about monogamy, and the possibilities for pleasurable sex outside a committed relationship? Again, what is the basis for judgments against them?

NOW resolutions dealing with sexual issues often reflect a shallow understanding of these topics. For example, a 1984 National resolution distinguishes between erotica, defined as that which is acceptable to women, from pornography, which is offensive to women and therefore condemned. In fact, any such distinction is subjective. Likewise, a 1980 position paper on lesbian rights mistakenly equates consensual sadomasochism with violence. Such resolutions reinforce narrow, traditional notions of women's desire as warm and fuzzy: nurturing, connected to intimacy, lacking in power dynamics, and unresponsive to explicit visual stimulus.

The Expertise of Sex Workers

For centuries, madonnas provided legitimate children and social respectability; whores, illegitimate pleasure. Proper women are socialized to associate sex with intimacy and often have difficulty negotiating their desires with men. Yet men are able to more easily distinguish between love and sex. They hold an advantage because they can enjoy erotic pleasure without the emotional restrictions so many women wrestle with. Our culture disproportionately discourages such behavior in women and will continue to do so until feminists claim such privileges for themselves. Why do women deny to each other the sexual freedom they allow men? What fears constrain them? Are we back to arguments that use biological determinism to justify behavior differences between the genders?

Some feminists want to know how sex work can be conducted in a manner that is not destructive or offensive to their dignity as women. They need to join with and listen to sexual service providers who are also interested in elevating themselves and their profession. This can be accomplished through both law reform and support of woman-friendly professional sex-worker organizations. Guilds and unions not forced underground because of legal constraints could promote ethical business practices, safer sex techniques, and responsible behavior.

Many women would like to know how to enhance their sex lives and relationships. They could benefit from associating with seasoned sex professionals, many of whom would gladly share their insights and expertise. Some examples of this can already be found in the San Francisco Bay Area, Los Angeles, and New York City, where current and former sex workers lead public forums, many designed specifically for women, sharing various erotic skills and challenging conventional ideas about sexuality and our bodies. These teachers are known as sacred prostitutes, mythologists, sex educators, or sensual masseuses. Their knowledge and expertise in the field of the erotic arts is sorely needed and should be highly valued. Instead, our culture uses sexual shame and ignorance for purposes of social control. The divisive sexual wounding of women—separating us into "madonnas" and "whores"—can heal. We must keep striving toward unity, working together for mutual benefit. What else can we do that makes any sense?

A Courtesan's Spiritual Calling

Amanda Brooks

Amanda Brooks notes that "courtesan" has been used differently in different eras, and while the word conjures up a rarefied sex worker, no one agrees on a courtesan's qualities. In her own work, Brooks was inspired by a book she borrowed from a friend, Kushiel's Dart, *by Jacqueline Carey. In the book, Carey describes a world without sexual prejudice, where courtesans—both male and female—work to obtain special skills. While many of these skills are sexual, they also consist of knowledge and spirituality. Brooks believes that courtesans working as prostitutes have the potential to fulfill a spiritual calling, one that achieves an "intimacy of spirit."*

I've participated on a particular public discussion forum way more than has been necessary. It's called the HDH (High Dollar Hotties) forum and concerns courtesans, paid companions, and those who simply charge higher-than-normal rates for their time. Scrolling through the forum one will read page after page of what defines a "courtesan," which nearly everyone seems to feel is the pinnacle of the "provider" spectrum.

When I worked, I aspired to be as courtesan-like as possible, using my own definitions, biases and prejudices. I know I didn't hit the mark all the time. If I did, I would've achieved my goal. Every escort uses her own definition of what a courtesan is, whether self-proclaimed or simply jumping into a discussion. And then we have to contend with the long history of courtesans, which vary from country to country and century to century. The word "courtesan" has been used to describe everything from a modern-day Nevada brothel employee to a handful of rarified newsmakers and trendsetters in

Amanda Brooks, "The Way of the Courtesan," *After Hours*, July 6, 2005. TexasGolden-Girl.com. Reproduced by permission.

19th century France and England. With such a wide range of concepts to choose from, what really is a courtesan?

Without a doubt, the word conjures images of rare beauty, impeccable grooming and poise, a sophisticated woman who is not worldly enough to be hard, charming, educated to the point of overkill, and able to captivate a man with a glance. There can be other qualities; such as being multi-lingual or a connoisseur of travel. She must be selective with her patrons and is always very expensive. The idea of sexual expertise is usually implied. Some self-described courtesans emphasize the romantic, lover-like quality they bring to each encounter. Others emphasize their wild sexual abandon. A certain agency in Australia is very upfront about the sexual techniques their courtesans are trained in, part of what they believe makes a courtesan a courtesan (and different from a mere escort).

None of these working definitions satisfied me. There was something lacking no matter how I twisted the combination around. And then I read a book [*Kushiel's Dart*, by Jacqueline Carey] that changed my perceptions forever.

Prostitution as a Religious Calling

By chance, I saw the cover on a friend's coffee table. Intrigued, I picked it up and read the back cover. Raging with curiosity, I borrowed the book and read it within 48 hours; not only being transported into this beautiful fantasy world but feeling the mystery of my profession solved in one fell swoop by a religious historian inspired to write about a headstrong, masochistic, courtesan [Phedre] I devoured the next two books in the series as soon as they were published. I've re-read these three books at least ten times each in the last three years, gleaning some new understanding every time (I'm a speed-reader).

The loveliest thing about the society in which Phedre lives in is the sexual freedom everyone enjoys. Her profession is considered a religious calling. Simply having a confirmed place in society makes such a big difference in the openness and honesty of the courtesans. Both men and women are freely accepted into training and as clients. There are thirteen "Houses" where the innate skills every adept has is honed into textbook perfection (and each house does indeed have its own code of desired perfection). And then there are the "street guilds" where perfection is probably less studiously attended to but the enthusiasm remains the same.

The mere idea of being able to freely pursue the perfection of my innate skills and talents with trained masters of my art is a heady one. But don't think that everything revolves around sex. The first thing all adepts learn to do is to kneel properly. Then they learn the art of serving food and drink. There is the study of history and religion and lessons in their art. Each house has its own art; such as massage, passion, domination, the arts (music, drawing, improv, acrobatics, etc.), and even honing a shrewd sense of finance. While this might be enough for most people, in this world, they go one step further.

Like I said, being a courtesan is considered a religious calling. Their goddess, Naamah, is so revered that none enter into the contract lightly. Adepts are asked if they wish to be dedicated to the service of their goddess. Only the willing are wanted. The contract between courtesan and patron is considered a religious pact. Breaking it is a crime and blasphemy. Patrons would never dream of leaving less than the contracted fee for the service or harming their courtesan. And the courtesans would never dream of giving less than everything their patrons desired.

Achieving an Intimacy of Spirit

Yes, I realize this is a fantasy world where sexual disease does not exist. However, I discovered the concepts translated quite beautifully. The idea of entering into every appointment with a whole-souled devotion (within my boundaries) was a final piece of the puzzle for me. I like the idea of service without being servile. I like to make someone happy. I am a perfectionist as well. Giving myself permission to be all that was a freeing experience for me. While I still had my 'image' that I marketed, more and more I turned to these books as a guide because these works of fiction gave me the internal response that was lacking when I read the discussion boards or others' definitions of a courtesan. There were no 'rules' of what a courtesan was or wasn't. By virtue of the fact that Phedre made the perfection of her calling her goal, she was a courtesan.

Another concept that attracted me was the idea that each person in the profession had some unique attribute that only they could contribute, if asked. Of course, there were standards of natural beauty and talent that had to be upheld to be a member of a house. Beyond that, every adept developed into their own person. Again, here was the intoxicating freedom to just be. A courtesan can only be the way she is by being a whole person.

I never believed I was worshipping a goddess. But when I felt I'd reached the ideal I'd created in my head, borne of these books, the feeling was completely fulfilling. It was more than a job well done. It was that my current place in this world [was] being filled as it should be. It was about being more. Not more than anyone else; but becoming more than myself for just a moment. It was a reaching out and connecting in a way that did not harm me or take anything from me. The books showed me a graceful way to strike the balance of professional and personal. Using all the facets of my being in a concentrated span of time created a wholeness that is lacking in everyday chores. Phedre states that she loves all of her patrons, even if just a little bit. I will say that's true for me too (except in the case of bad clients). Courtesan-ship is not the intimacy of bodies, as so many believe, but the intimacy of spirit.

I'm still amazed that it took a book of fiction, written by someone who has zero experience in the adult industry, to perfectly capture the beauty of the profession, with no prejudice or taint, and then improve upon it like nothing I've ever read. I owe Carey a debt of thanks for giving me a tangible, attainable ideal. I'm still digesting and learning from these books, even in my personal life. Phedre learns something new about the mystery of the service of Naamah every year of her life. I can expect no less for myself.

In the second book, Phedre is given the opportunity to perfectly reveal what she is all about. A foreign prince mocks her chosen profession. He sneers that for a price she will pretend interest in him. She responds, ". . .for a price, I will pretend absolutely nothing."

Sex Workers Are Feminists

Gillette

Gillette realizes that she has a tendency to make feminists angry because she is a sex worker who does not believe that her occupation is degrading. At one time, Gillette was a hardcore feminist who disliked men, but over time she changed her views: she had grown tired of seeing herself as a victim. Calling oneself a victim simply allows other people (those who have victimized you) to have power. One's power should come from within. Gillette also disliked how feminists insisted that everyone conform to a certain set of beliefs. Feminists who are prejudiced against prostitutes are wrong: sex workers are feminists, because they have made, and live by, their own choices.

The reason I generally piss off feminists isn't only because I'm a sex worker who's proud to stand and say what she's done. It's because they don't usually appreciate my flavor of Feminism and my viewpoint on the prevailing form of Feminism. Because it's like talking about Religion and Politics and Abortion, I generally shy away from the conversation as I get tired of the lightning that comes my way. But, oh well ... I'm stepping out these days so will again here.

Does escorting help or set back Feminism? I don't think it does either. Or maybe it does both, depending on the situation. I guess I'm kind of frustrated and sad that the question needs to be asked because I'm frustrated and sad about Feminism in general. And on so, So, SO many levels I don't really care about the discussion any more as I did enough of it years ago. I'm over talking about it because I decided instead to quietly *do*.

Wow ... until about fifteen years ago, I would never in a gazzillion years have thought those words would ever come

Gillette, "Feminism and Sex Work," *Ex-Courtesan in Transition (Again)*, July 29, 2007. http://ex-courtesan.blogspot.com/search/label/Feminism. Reproduced by permission.

out of my mouth. I was a radical, Patriarchy Hating Feminist for more years of my life than not. I blamed men for their evil plan when they created The Patriarchy and its ultimate cause for every ill on the planet. Even jello was part of the sinister master plan (joke). I had a vision of communities where only women and children lived. For sex, we would bus in a load of men from time to time ... then they would go away, leaving the rest of us to live in harmony and peace. I *knew* that anyone who didn't understand the One True dynamics of the world was either blind, ignorant, foolish or puppets ... or some other awful thing. I was so vocal and militant about it, many people noticed. I was labeled a Man Hater by more than one observer....

But I went through a huge transformation in my personality and outlook on life. It led me from being a Man Hater to a Whore who decided to participate *with* men in *our* healing. Part of that journey was looking at myself and my feminist ways and how destructive they were to me and, in my opinion, all of us.

No Longer a Victim

I got tired of seeing myself as a *Victim*.

I learned that I cannot become empowered by tenaciously clinging to my Victimhood. Every time I speak about how I have been "wronged" as a woman, I am declaring and reinforcing my victimhood. Singing the I AM A VICTIM song over and over and over until it's embedded in every brain synapse does not lead to a strong vision of the self. It might give the outer illusion of strength, as anger and loud bitching often can. But the loudest shouter is not the person of power. They have to shout so they look powerful to cover up the fact that they don't believe they have any at all.

How in the hell does a VICTIM be truly powerful? A very different "battle" ensues when it originates from a place of *standing* in my power rather than screaming for the world to change itself so that my Victim can feel safe.

I don't know what the lingo of today's feminist is. When I was mucking around in that world, one of the battle cries was a yearning to revisit the definition of "power" from that of "power over" to "power within." When a battle is fought by a Victim, they fight in a way to regain "power over." When a truly powerful woman stands in her own light and follows her Path, she beams a power from within. It's that power that will ultimately win the day because it's centered and balanced and knows itself. It doesn't create more enemies, blaming everything around it for its situation. It builds bridges to find a common way to resolution. This Power just quietly goes about its business, following where it's led to impact the immediate world around it. It knows that change starts *right here*. It decides to let Victims scream the big, loud song and knows that nothing much gets done on that level because Victim operates in a way that separates.

Conformist Feminism

Women don't exist to support Feminism. Feminism exists to support women. When women remain Victims, they need to have others around to support their feelings of "rightness." If someone disagrees with their "club" they become "the enemy" and lose that club's support. Lines are drawn, the battle ensues, with Victim demeaning Other to make its point (dirty battle tactics of someone with no internal sense of power). All the while the one who thinks differently just asks for the right to exist as they choose. Victim requires that everyone have its point of view. It needs the support of the club to survive. The club is the only place it can find strength because it has none itself.

If a woman, say like a Whore, challenges that viewpoint they come under the crossfire. Victim clings tenaciously to the rightness of its position and need to crush, ostracize the 'other,' to maintain that position. I keep wondering how feminism supports women when it takes this tactic. I certainly don't see that it does. What I get is the message that we all have to conform to the standard MO [modus operandi] or we are attacked more fervently than "the Patriarchy." I thought this was the antithesis of what Feminism is supposed to stand for. I understand the dynamic and need for that within the Victim mind-set (must squash those close dissenters to solidify our position) but refuse to support the machine that creates it.

When feminists finally and fully embrace their power from within, they won't have anything to say to women who choose to be sex-workers. They won't care because they will feel so strong internally that they won't feel threatened by women who make a choice different than the ones they make.

I understand it's easy to have the Victim's mind-set. There's lots out there that isn't pretty. But to be truly effective, I found that I needed to make the choice to change my perspective and *see* differently. This Whore's message to Feminists is to please let Victim Go. Or don't . . . your choice and I will support you in that choice. If you find seeing yourself as a Victim as productive or that it makes you happy, go for it with my full blessings. But if you want to find peace within yourself, quit requiring that I look at myself as one because I won't go there with you. If you keep focusing on me, I'm only going to piss you off . . . and what's the point of that? Life's too damn short and precious to spend so much of it being pissed.

I see you as my Sister. I wish you could see me as yours and treat me like one.

Are Sex Workers Feminists?

So back to the original question: Does Escorting help or set back feminism? Just for fun, let's say both.

Sex Work *does* set back Feminism in that it gives some Angry Feminists the opportunity to judge other women, divide women and sing the Victim song a little louder in yet another area. And since in Victim mode we need to have someone to blame, let's just point out that this isn't the "fault" of escorts, but rather the Feminst's choice to separate and judge their sisters.

Sex Work *doesn't* set back Feminism in that it has no impact on any individual or movement unless the individual or movement decides to let it do that to them. Much as I wish I could wave my magic wand, I can't control your feeling like a victim.

Sex workers *are* Feminists in that we're women standing for our choices no matter how anyone else around us says we should be acting or conducting our lives. We refuse to listen to the Religious Right, to judgmental people in the Harper Valley PTA, arrogant people who decide they know what's best for us because of how "sick" we must be, *and* Angry Feminists. That would be my brand of Feminism—the one that I live and that remains my commitment today.

As . . . I have no idea who will be reading this, thus which buttons will get pushed creating a person *unable to hear what I'm saying*, I want to state very clearly that I abhor the idea of prostitution anywhere. My definition of prostitution is where anyone does anything they don't want to do just for the money, whether it's selling their body, a vacuum cleaner, or their time sitting at a computer terminal . . . and obviously Trafficking Women is in a different league than selling a vacuum, OK? These are not feminist issues . . . they are societal issues, humanist issues. They are neither the same thing nor the same discussion of a woman or man who chooses to become a sex-worker and that decision's impact on feminism. OK?

CHAPTER 3

The Consequences
of Prostitution

Memoirs of a Hollywood Prostitute

David Henry Sterry, as told to Daniel Maurer

At the age of seventeen, David Henry Sterry became a "rent boy," a respected and well-paid prostitute in Hollywood. After leaving prostitution behind, however, he exhibited self-destructive behaviors. To help himself recall and heal from his experience as a prostitute, he eventually wrote a memoir, Chicken: Self-Portrait of a Young Man for Rent *and began performing* Chicken: A 1-Ho Show. *While writing his memoir had negative side effects (e.g., alienating his father), it also allowed him to become a spokesperson for the rights of sex workers. By reliving his experience as a rent boy through his memoir and his stage show, Sterry was able to heal his emotional wounds. Chicken has also been optioned for potential development by HBO.*

When he was 17-years-old, David Henry Sterry left his suburban childhood to attend a Catholic college in Hollywood. As it turned out, the place didn't have dorms. And he only had $27 in his pocket. His parents were too distracted to help. Not that David, whose teenage mantra was "whatever," knew how to ask. The first person he talked to in Hollywood—an anonymous man with a T-shirt that read "Sexxy"—offered him a steak, took him back to his house, and raped and robbed him, setting him on a path that quickly led to a seven-month career as a male prostitute.

Chicken: Self-Portrait of a Young Man for Rent, is not a dark, brooding memoir. From the first page, Sterry writes with the mordant, jagged wit of [novelist] Chuck Palahniuk. Sterry's encounters range from the cliché—there's the "take-no-

Daniel Maurer, "Grilling the Chicken: Q & A with David Sterry, Former Rent Boy," *Black Table*, January 12, 2005. www.blacktable.com/maurier050111.htm. Reproduced by permission.

prisoners, lifestyles-of-the-rich-and-famous, old-fashioned, newfangled orgy"—to the truly horrifying.

After leaving the sex business, Sterry, while outwardly successful (he has starred in over 500 television commercials), struggled with what he calls self-destructive behavior.

Chicken was published in 2002. While on the book tour, Sterry, who has a background in commercial acting, discovered a love for performing the material and evolved it into a "1 ho show" that he has since performed in Belgium, Australia, England, New York, and his hometown of San Francisco. Stephen Hopkins ("24") is slated to direct [it as] a miniseries for HBO. The Black Table interviewed Sterry, while he was in New York City preparing to pitch the stage play to producers.

Black Table: You've said that you revised this book 40 times. Why did it take so long to get right? Was it a cathartic process?

David Henry Sterry: This was my first book, and I was flying by the seat of my pants. I was fortunate enough that my agent—who is now my wife—loves editing. We did draft after draft, partly because the subject matter was so personal that I had no objectivity with it. The first draft was very bitter. The writing was very dark, relentless—and then there would be a joke. She really helped me to take a lot of that out of it, because nobody wants to read that, however cathartic it may be to write. The subject matter is dark enough as it is. Also it became clear these little snippets from childhood were a good device to give readers a break and let them breathe for a second. I wrote 100 pages of that stuff, but it was difficult to figure out where to put these things. I wanted them to sort of illuminate what had just happened, but at that the same time I hate it when authors tell the readers what they're supposed to think.

Do you feel the end product is as honest as that first draft? Are there things that you regret were left out in order to make the book more [sellable]?

There was one scene where I was basically given as a birthday present to an 82-year-old woman [by one of her friends]. One of the chief differences between male and female sex workers is this: there are a lot of things in life you can fake, but an erection is just not one of them. I was terrified that I wouldn't be able to perform for this woman, because she was so old. When you're seventeen, everybody seems like either old or almost dead. But as it turned out, she didn't seem 82 to me—she was vibrant, with it. She was dressed very stylishly. She had a couple of glasses of champagne, so she was kind of tipsy. She treated me so nicely, and so respectfully and sweetly. And she was just adorable. She said that through her whole life, she had fantasized about having someone kiss her "down there." She couldn't even say the word. She was very appreciative and responsive. I was never quite sure why it had to come out [of the book]—they thought it was too weird. Which is so odd to me, given some of the weird things in the book. My main regret is that my idea at the time was to write about the most extreme things that happened, and in retrospect I wish I had included more of the mundane, meat-and-potatoes jobs. The jobs I wrote about were exceptions.

Who were the meat-and-potatoes clients?

Quite a few business women from out of town, and then a lot of rich, bored housewives. Normal, not pretty, not ugly, not fat, not thin—you couldn't pick them out of a crowd. The only thing they had in common was that they all had money.

Has publishing the story removed you from it—does it feel like your own story when you tell it, or does it feel like something that happened to someone else? Is it weird to objectify this experience?

It was very helpful to do that. It helped to clarify in my own mind what these events meant to me, and how they resonated throughout the rest of my life. For many years I had a lot of difficulty even saying these things out loud, and I hid them from everyone I knew. I was ashamed. But writing was so cathartic—it enabled me to come to peace with it. I used to have terrible nightmares about Sexxy. But as soon as I started portraying him on stage, all these fantasies just disappeared. That was the ultimate revenge—making art out of this stuff. I get e-mails almost every day, a lot of them from 18-year-old girls who had terrible things happen to them, and when I do shows or events every single time there are people who come up to me and tell me their horrible, miserable story about how somebody f---ed them when they were a kid. A lot of times you can tell they've never said this stuff out loud. They know I'm not going to call them a freak because I'm the poster boy for freaks now. It never occurred to me this would happen, but it's so liberating to let people get all of this out of them.

Do you ever regret living such a public life? Are there things you [wish you] hadn't put on the record?

The only thing that is slightly problematic is when people assume they can ask you anything. My wife is a very private person, so when people ask me about my personal sexual life with my wife, that's a little troubling. There have been severe repercussions for going public with this—for outing myself. A good portion of my family doesn't speak to me. But it has also shown me who my real friends are. And it's opened this whole new world of people. I've traveled the world with this book. I just came back from Amsterdam and I have an Amsterdam crew now. All these smart, funny, alternative, freaky people. For every person that has said something nasty to me, there have been a hundred great things that came into my life. It's how I got the love of my life—my wife.

You mentioned your family. The book portrays your parents as absent and not caring, but in the acknowledgments you thank them for their love and support. What did they think about the way you portrayed them? How much did you think about their reaction as you wrote?

Again, this is where Ariel (his wife) was incredibly helpful. I did have a very happy childhood, I really did. My family was dysfunctional certainly, but no more so than anybody else's. We weren't beaten, we always had clothes, we were encouraged to do what we wanted, we were read to. That's part of what helped me survive, and I'm thankful for that. A lot of those kids in that world didn't have any parents, they went from institution to institution and were beaten. A lot of them are dead or drug addicts. Ariel was instrumental in saying let's write some nice things about your childhood. I went out of my way to write about my father taking me to baseball games, my mother encouraging me to be happy in life. I felt that was very important. I also wanted to dispel the myth that every person who goes into sex work was beaten and raped in childhood. It's a misconception. I was meticulous to mention an equal combination of things that were nice and not nice. As careful as I was, my father believes that this book is nothing but one long, relentless attack on him. The second the manuscript was accepted, I sent a copy to everyone in my family. My father was furious—he felt it made him look like a monster. I don't think it makes him look like that at all—I just feel like it makes him look like at that age, he was going through a terrible time. His wife walked out on him. He went through a horrible divorce, which is really debilitating. My mother was figuring out how to live with her new lover. I was bitter and angry for a long time, and a lot of that did come out in the first draft, but I really was careful to take as much of it as I could out of it. It became clear to me that I didn't ask for the help that I needed. It was a great opportunity for me to go from being victimized by someone else to accepting responsibility for my actions. I wasn't forced to be a prostitute—no one put a gun to my head. Yeah, I was young and stupid, but it was still my young, stupid choice. I could've walked away at any moment. I wanted to make that clear. My mother and I are great friends now. She came to see the show—she says she hasn't read the book—and she was so appreciative and generous with her praise. She said ok I understand now in a way that I didn't before.

You say at some point in the book that after you left the business, you tried to capture the excitement of it by acting out in various ways. Obviously part of you was being dragged back.

It is an exciting world. You feel like a rock star. You get tons of respect, money, nobody f---s with you. When I was in that world, I was a star, everyone knew me, I had a reputation, all these friends, people who admired me, a position in life. When I was on the job I usually felt powerful, unless someone was being ugly and mean to me, and like I was worth $100 an hour (about $350 in today's money) compared to $20 an hour frying chicken. There's a real power in feeling successful in that world. You don't realize the emotional toll at the time.

How does that knowledge of the emotional toll and the dubious motivations translate to your current work with sex workers?

I was just in Amsterdam meeting with sex-worker activists and academics who are organizing a huge conference in October and it looks like I'm going to help write this manifesto that is going to be sent to the governments of the world. I never felt under threat because I was bigger than most of my clients, but that's not the case with a lot of the women I'm friends with. Almost everyone I know who has worked on the streets has been raped, and often by the cops. So first and foremost, I want to make sure that if you're an adult and you come to the consciousness that this is what you want to do to make your money—this is the best way to use your talents— that you can ply your trade and be safe. In Amsterdam, you have this great model of the windows—there is no violence. There are trafficked people in Amsterdam, people from third world countries. But where it has been decriminalized, violence has been eliminated. I also want to raise awareness that kids are being used in sex—by judges, lawyers, doctors, people who are pillars of society. People don't fully understand this.

Quite a few people who do sex work aren't so articulate and haven't been to college, and I feel like I can be a voice. And there aren't a lot of men who speak out about this also.

What is performing the play like?

It's one of the funnest things I do in my life. I play myself as the 17-year-old narrator. I play about 10 other characters from the book. [I]t's very different than the book because it's very visual. It's full of laughs. There'll be a huge laugh and the next second there will be something so jarring and weird and off-putting that you can hear people holding their breath. I love stuff that walks the edge, where you're laughing one second and then you're going "oh my god." It's interesting, you don't get to see who reads your book. But I get to see every motherf---er who comes to the play—a lot of 18-year-old girls, and it's weird, but this is a date show. A lot of couples come. I get a lot of gay men who come because they think *Chicken* is a gay thing. At first I was nervous about that because the climax is me beating a gay man to a pulp, but a lot of the gay guys I talk to have worked in the sex business. They just see it as a boy's coming-of-age story, as opposed to gay/straight/whatever. That gave me faith for the world. Then I have a lot of middle aged women, who are in some ways the subject of the show. In Scotland I had this grandmother come up to me—she was like 100 years old—who said to me [in a little old lady voice], "Do you mind if I give you a wee kiss." She kissed me on the cheek and said "Now I can say I've kissed a gigolo." It was so sweet. I was like, ok, she got it. I was worried this would be a sort of angsty, avant garde crowd. But this review in the *Chronicle* said this show is for anyone who has ever had or been a child. In a way it is about being a kid—what could happen to your kid if you're not careful. So the show has been a blessing.

What was the rave like? What was it like performing this play in the rent boy capital of the world?

It was incredible. It was in the middle of the woods and they built this 20-ft paper mache head, kind of like Burning Man [an annual festival that takes place in Black Rock City, Nevada]. Everybody was on ecstasy, and they insisted I take it before my performance, but I wouldn't know how to do it. Imagine a group of 600 Amsterdamers on ecstasy, and then they gave me 5 girls to perform with. These Nordic Dutch goddess looking girls. They told me I could do whatever I wanted with them. I had a big chorus—I would say a line and they would repeat the line and act it out behind me. And there was this big orgasm scene, where the girls were all orgasming behind me. And the whole crowd was orgasming. It was one of the highlights of my performing career. I did 12 shows in 15 days in Amsterdam. The reaction was great. They were very relaxed, open, warm. They treat writers differently in Europe. They revere the writer. You're treated like a star. I was very touched by the generosity that I was shown there. As a writer in America, you aren't used to that. People were much more excited when my book was optioned by HBO.

Given that you're now shooting for a 9-month stint in New York, do you think you'll ever retire the act?

That's the joke around my house—I'll be 85 years old and saying (in old man's voice) "I was a chicken!"

A Downward Spiral

Cecelia Wardlaw

Growing up as an American Catholic in the conservative 1950s, Wardlaw never imagined herself becoming a prostitute. But she found marriage dissatisfying and eventually, after leaving her husband, discovered that she preferred women to men. After meeting a woman whom she fell in love with, the couple moved into a house together. But instead of living the American Dream, they both became addicted to drugs, and Wardlaw worked regularly as a prostitute to pay the bills. Over time, however, the relationship became strained, and after several suicide attempts, Wardlaw realized that she had to leave. Wardlaw has also written an essay for Early Embraces: True Life Stories of Women Describing Their First Lesbian Experience.

I was born forty-eight years ago to a Roman Catholic and alcoholic family. I am a recovering addict, and I recently learned that I was an incest victim.

As I was growing up, I remember poring over any books which offered me information about sex. My mother hid the medical books I was reading, so I retreated to dictionaries and encyclopedias which I found at the library. As a young teenager in the 1950's, I tried unsuccessfully to seduce the neighborhood boys. They, too, were Roman Catholics, and Roman Catholics in the era of "Father Knows Best" saved themselves for marriage. In 1960, I was a virgin bride and hot as hell. My husband could not match my sexual appetite, and I thought the problem was due to some fault of mine. I began reading again. I found sex manuals, which were relatively new then, but my husband said they gave me "too many ideas." When articles about massage parlors first appeared in magazines, I

Cecelia Wardlaw, "Dream Turned Nightmare," *Sex Work: Writings by Women in the Sex Industry*, San Francisco: Cleis Press, 1998. Copyright © 1987, 1998 by Frédérique Delacoste and Priscilla Alexander. All rights reserved. Reproduced by permission.

was fascinated. I fantasized about what it would be like to be a prostitute, but thought my chances of ever becoming one were slim. Little did I know.

As my children grew older, I became more involved in their lives and my own expanded. I began doing volunteer work in the community and found people who thought the way I did. I found support for my ideas. I also discovered I loved women. My life was full and content. Even sex was not as frustrating.

Then we were transferred to the south.

I remember kneeling in front of the Blessed Mother's statue that first evening in our new city, and sobbing. A few weeks later, on our twelfth anniversary, my husband and I went out to dinner. I remember sitting across the table from him, thinking, "I have nothing in common with you."

Leaving Home

It took me a year to work up the courage to leave.

When I eventually left, I discovered that I had not the faintest idea about living alone and taking care of myself. Alcohol and pills entered my life. It took at least one joint to work up the courage I needed to go into a bar. The men I met just wanted sex. Free sex. I went along with that, but not for long. In the meantime, a woman I had grown to love while I was still married came to visit me. Our first night together, we got high, laughed and talked about old times. The second night, we made love. Then she left. I didn't know what to do. I was far too timid to go to a gay bar, even high.

I was a registered nurse and worked in a methadone maintenance center as a nurse/therapist. Just as the magazine articles about prostitution fascinated me, tales of the streets and street life now caught my attention. In my vulnerable state, it did not take me very long to become romantically involved with one of my male patients. I began stealing drugs for him. My man ended up in the penitentiary, and I was once again on my own.

I found my way back to the north, and ended up back in the bars. I began turning tricks, not so much to make money, but to avoid giving away sex. I met a woman who was street-wise, beautiful, shot drugs, and wanted to be with me. I was in love. She introduced me to heroin, and, for the first time, I developed a physical dependency.

Linda and I lived together in a house I had bought just to get her under my roof. Once I became addicted to heroin, there were two habits to support and we needed more money. My criminal activity increased and, in time, I was arrested. After I was released from jail, we needed fast money, badly. I was no longer employable as a registered nurse, and besides, the money was too slow in coming. We sat down one day with the phone book, looking for massage parlors, and found several. Linda's cousin and I went out the next day to check them out.

Becoming a Prostitute

The parlors weren't located in the best section of town. At the first one, we climbed a dark, dismal stairway to the second floor where we found a hulk of a man sitting at a desk. He glared as we approached him. There were five or six scantily clad women lounging in a variety of poses on couches and chairs. They all smiled as we entered. The man instructed us to fill out an index card with our names, addresses, and phone numbers, and said that he would call us.

The next parlor was further uptown, on a street laden with bars. Again, we climbed to the second floor of a seedy looking building. This time we were told to return that night at 11:00 to see the manager.

We went back to the street and entered a pick-up place. I perched on a bar stool, and soon, a man began playing with my leg. A voice said, "Watch it." I turned to the door and saw a monster-sized cop. I slid off the bar stool, and told Linda's cousin I was heading home. She decided to stay and try her luck at another joint. She called us later that night from jail. She had been arrested.

I returned to the parlor at 11:00. I was told to go down a hallway—even darker and more dismal than the stairway—and into a back room to take off my clothes. In the room I found a bed made up with a single sheet and a towel. The walls were covered with mirrors. What little plaster was exposed was painted black and red. I stripped down to my panty hose and blouse. The manager knocked on the door, told me to remove the rest of my clothes, and left. When he returned, he laid down, after removing his clothing, and told me to sit down, indicating the edge of the bed. He told me to do anything I liked. I remember looking at him questioningly, but got no further instruction from him. I shrugged my shoulders and began handling his genitals. I gave him head. He tapped me on the shoulder and told me that I had done fine, and that I should report for work in the morning. I was so relieved. Since my release from jail, Linda and I had no source of income except welfare checks and the few tricks I was able to turn. I did not want Linda to whore. My skin crawled at the thought of her being touched by a man.

I turned up late on my first day in the parlor. As soon as I got home the night before, Linda and I got high, and we continued until morning when we ran out of drugs. I had to wait for her to get more so that I could make it through the day. I guess that by the time I arrived at work, the women really weren't expecting me. They looked surprised when I came into the room.

First Day of the Job

I was sent to a dressing room, with a dresser, a bald light bulb hanging overhead, and hooks on the wall for street clothes. As many as six women at a time used this room—which measured only about eight by ten feet—to change clothes. Next door was a laundry room with washers and dryers that ran continuously. The parlor never closed, and we were frequently on the floor for sixteen hours without a break.

Apparently I was taking too long in the dressing room, because a beautiful black woman was sent after me. They thought I was shy, or afraid. In fact, I was so high I couldn't move very fast and I was unnecessarily repeating a lot of motions.

I made it to the front sitting room and took the last seat on the couch. The women engaged in small talk until Daisy, who worked the desk, observed a john through a strategically placed mirror outside the steel, electronic door. When Daisy called, "Customer," a flurry of activity ensued. Women sat up straight, applied lipstick, pulled up or pulled down clothing, smiled on command, and struck seductive poses—all in a matter of seconds.

Customers came and went all day, and I remained unchosen. When a man was buzzed in, he approached the desk, exchanged a few words with Daisy, and pulled out some money. Then he turned to us, and we smiled and struck poses. I learned all of this by observation. No one gave me any verbal instructions, although I was sent in on a few sessions that first day to watch. The john would select a woman, who would lead him to a large, gaudily decorated room. Large mirrors were standard, walls were painted in dark reds, blues, greens and black, and there was plenty of gilded trim on walls, mirrors, and bathroom fixtures. Most rooms included a large, raised bathtub, used for the most expensive sessions, which lasted an hour. Standard sessions began at fifteen minutes for a hand job at twenty-five dollars, or half-and-half [intercourse and oral sex] at forty dollars. Prices and times varied according to the desires of the customers. The longest session available was one hour, included the use of the tub and a half-and-half, at one hundred dollars. English sessions (s/m) [sado-masochism] were strictly tailored both in cost and content by the desires and pocketbooks of the customers. Only certain women did s/m sessions, and I was told early on that I would be good at it. I think it was because I looked so angry.

I remained unchosen well into that first evening, until a very high young man was buzzed in. All of the other women were busy with customers. He sat, or rather, fell to the couch beside me, and I began talking to him. Before I knew it, I had him talked into a hundred dollar session. I became the favorite of the "drunk crowd" after that. I wasn't afraid of them and found I could talk them into just about anything.

Hitting Bottom

Several months after I began working, very early one morning, an extremely intoxicated man was buzzed into the room. He ended up spending the rest of the night with me and subsequently became a regular customer. I had several regulars by this time and even was occasionally the "top booker." My trips to the street were far less frequent, but life at home was getting worse and worse.

Linda said that her lack of interest in sex was due to her increasing dependence on heroin. I suspected it was due to my sexual involvement with men. When I would try to quit my work, she would pick a fight, and I would end up getting beaten.

Money was a constant problem. There was just never enough. If I made two hundred or two thousand a week—and it varied that much—the money disappeared. That's how we arrived at Christmas of that year with no money. Our Christmas dinner consisted of a half pound of ham and three scrambled eggs. We were both sick—dope sick. Linda said that if we weren't together, we'd each be having a merry Christmas. She always said that it was our racial difference that caused us problems. I knew that it was drugs. I was in such denial that I remember wishing for Santa Claus to magically appear before morning with a tree and train. He didn't, of course, and I never felt so stuck in my life.

The months lumbered on. I lost my house because no mortgage payments had been made for over fourteen months. We moved to an apartment and I began seeing my early morning visitor on my own time. I lived with constant paranoia. Eventually I was fired from the parlor. I was taking too much time off work and coming in beaten. This is a very difficult period for me to put on paper, although I talk about it a lot. Losing my house was deadening. When I bought my house—during a period of sobriety in 1980—I was the proudest woman around. I had so many hopes for Linda and me. Losing my house meant losing all hope that she and I would work out our life together.

After I was fired, I managed to land a nursing position with a temporary agency. I was also seeing my john three or four times a week. Money was better than ever, but life was hell. My john was paying the rent, buying the groceries and giving me two hundred dollars each time I saw him. I was on methadone, which meant that my physical need for heroin was no longer a factor. Linda and I fought constantly about that fact. I was being beaten regularly and made several feeble attempts at suicide.

There was one counselor at the meth clinic whom I would call whenever I had been brutally beaten. She said, "When you've had enough, you'll do something about it." And I did. It took months, but I did leave.

Living as an HIV-Positive Porn Star and Escort

Tony Valenzuela

At one point in his life, Tony Valenzuela lived with a triple threat to any new relationship: he was HIV positive, a porn star, and an escort. He believed he had inherited his father's promiscuous nature, though unlike his father, Valenzuela was gay. When he first learned he was HIV positive, however, his life changed. After two years of depression, he attempted to live a normal life, only to be stuck in a boring retail job. He decided to become a prostitute and found steady work in Los Angeles. Although he realized that his career as an escort and porn star made relationships difficult, he nonetheless began one. After the relationship failed, he decided that the best way to deal with his triple-threat status was to tell a potential boyfriend the truth at the very beginning. Through his own honesty, he learned that others were willing to trust him, despite his background.

Prostitution is a complicated business. At times I'm beside myself with the ease of it all—the amount of money I make, the freedom it gives me to sit at Starbucks in West Hollywood and cruise boys anytime I want, the places I travel to, things I buy, restaurants I'm taken to. . . . And then I can't wait to get out of it, feeling like I'd rather throw myself into traffic than have to turn another trick. Hooking makes dating next to impossible, and I get frustrated that it cuts into my personal sex life.

It's a crazy, f---d-up world that I'm proud to partake in, as when I worked my ass off through college as a waiter. But this is far more special. The motivations, risks, and sacrifices are

Tony Valenzuela, "A Complicated Business," *Tricks and Treats: Sex Workers Write About Their Clients* Binghamton, NY: Haworth Press, 2000. Copyright © 2000 by The Haworth Press, Inc. All rights reserved. Reproduced by permission.

high drama. The payoff, at times, simply glamorous. The freedom has been nothing less than lifesaving. Every whore has his own story. . . .

The evening I launched my career as a high-priced homosexual prostitute (as the media used to call Andrew Cunanan, the gay serial killer), I was sitting alone, painfully bored and frustrated at the part-time minimum-wage job I'd taken in a small clothing store in Hillcrest. I had just come out of the longest depression of my life, and the retail job was my reintroduction to responsibility. Two years prior, at age twenty-six, I learned I'd become HIV positive. My infection bulldozed my already crumbling idealism, and, eventually, the career I'd carefully built throughout my twenties as a professional gay activist collapsed. Facing one's mortality is a hard and fast lesson in cutting through bullshit. I couldn't take the rank smell of a sterilized gay movement any longer. Furthermore, the loneliness of the changed epidemic for someone of my generation forced me into a solitary process of grieving for a life that felt destroyed, yet showed no signs of destruction—no KS [Kaposi's Sarcoma] lesions, no memorial services for my best friends, no surprise obituaries, not even a Quilt to help release the tears I felt guilty to shed in public.

Writing about the anguish of telling my parents, or the recurring feelings of hopelessness that I would die young, or my battle to get the gay community to understand the complexities of sexual risk taking in an evolving and unyielding epidemic—these are heavy subjects to skim over in order to have the space to recount even a slice of my career in sex work. They were experiences that consumed two dark years of my life that I pushed through with a morbid sense of humor, like belly laughing over every issue of *Diseased Pariah News* or wanting to title my first book *HIV Positive and LOVING IT!*, with a picture of an ecstatic me on the cover doing a jig. Above all, I got through that time with the loving support of a few friends and a dear, remarkable family.

Like Father, Like Son

I often look back at my family's history to try to pull up how its values influenced my sexual exploration. My father, who is Mexican, is a Latino through and through when it comes to sex. He was quite a playboy when he was young, and marriage didn't seem to taper his wandering libido. Observing my father, I sometimes shudder to think what kind of smooth-talking womanizer I might have become had I been straight. Instead, I was lucky enough to be part of a group of people (gay men) who view sexual conquest as a community value rather than a victory over weakness.

I was already predisposed to hustling. Sex has been a sweeping and defining theme in my life, almost epic in my adulthood. The two great crises of my life, homosexuality and HIV, both have very much to do with sex. Sex has been an obsessive fascination of mine, like food and cooking are to my mother, who is constantly poring over culinary books and magazines, always trying new recipes and perfecting old ones. She owns an Italian restaurant. I opened a one-man brothel.

My background is Third World and Old World (immigrant Mexican on my father's side, first-generation Italian on my mother's), but with a First World sense of entitlement. In other words, the Valenzuelas have made their way through America expecting everyone else to think the way we do.

"Wives need to understand the service that prostitutes provide to a marriage," my fifty-seven-year-old mother said loudly at a family gathering a couple of years back. Not to misunderstand her, my mom is actually a sexual prude. One time she asked me what a ménage à trois was, and when I told her, she responded, wide-eyed and horrified, "That's disgusting!" But she's also wise to the world of Monica Lewinsky and Bill Clinton. When I told her nervously that I'd made my first porn movie, the first thing she asked was how much money I got for it. She has a strong live-and-let-live attitude about most things, even with her children.

"I've never met a prostitute I didn't like," she stated with conviction, as the rest of the family munched on chips and seviche.

"Neither has Dad!" my sister screamed. We all roared with laughter.

In situations such as these with my family, I think it's no wonder I am how I am. And it's no wonder I'm a snag in the fabric of rigid values in American society. To live honestly about one's sexual desires and behaviors is an assault to most people who unabashedly lie about their sex lives and sexual fantasies.

Venturing into Sex Work

That fateful evening at the clothing store, I was resolved to simplify my life economically and venture into sex work, which had long been a burning curiosity. I decided that I would drive up to LA and check out the fabled hooker bar Numbers, where several of my friends had met their sugar daddies. To avoid the hassle of anyone trying to talk me out of this decision, I began my profession without telling a soul. I didn't know where the bar was, so I dialed Los Angeles information for the number. I realized I couldn't ask if this was the bar where hustlers hooked up with clients, so I said to the man who answered the phone, "I'm calling from San Diego, and is this the bar that has that *very interesting reputation* for its clientele?" "Yes, it is," he answered, with a chuckle. I asked for directions.

After a two-hour drive up from San Diego, I arrived at Numbers, which was then on Sunset Boulevard, at around 10:30 p.m. I didn't even know what to wear or how the procedure worked. I kept telling myself that I wouldn't be ashamed if I ran into anyone I knew, though I prayed that I wouldn't. Like all of my escort friends, I made up a pseudonym. Although I didn't understand making up a name for something that required me being seen, I made one up anyway. I came up with "Marco" because I look Mediterranean and because it seemed exotic and sexy.

I parked my car a couple of blocks away from the bar. Still sitting in the driver's seat, I pulled on skintight black vinyl pants and a tight black shirt. A hustler should look like a hustler, I thought. In truth, one of my sexual fantasies was to feel like a hooker. I would soon realize how much I got off on the idea of being bought, being someone's piece of ass for an hour or an evening. It was a turn-on, especially when the client treated me like "his whore.". . . Unfortunately, I'd learn that most clients weren't into playing my cheap hooker fantasy scenes. It was about them, not me. Though, oftentimes, they'd tell me it was important I was getting pleasure also ("Oh, of course. It feels great . . ." I'd say as I left my body).

Numbers had smoked-glass mirrored walls as you walked in, with a bathroom immediately to the right. I checked myself out in the full length of the mirrors, turning around to inspect my butt. I stopped in the restroom to kill a little time. The restroom was tiny and crowded, and it was completely obvious who would be buying and who would be selling downstairs at the bar. I waited my turn for the mirror. As everyone stared at me, I self-consciously looked at the whites of my eyes, my teeth, fussed a bit with my hair.

Learning the Business

There was a young guy, one of the hookers, I presumed, at the urinal talking to an older man who was peering over his shoulder at the guy's dick, commenting on its enormous size. Two other men took a peek, and the younger guy peeing seemed to enjoy the attention. A disturbing feeling of embarrassment came over me, like he was a white-trash prostitute for letting them look. All the while, I wanted to look, too, but didn't, and I was no better, wearing pants so tight anyone could tell I wasn't wearing underwear.

With my heart pounding hard in my chest, I walked down the flight of stairs that descended into the bar. I'd forgotten that Numbers was also a restaurant. It was dimly lit and smoky. The floor was jammed with young guys and older men, either standing around or sitting at the tables that surrounded the bar area. It took about one minute for me to run into someone from San Diego, who, by his age and outfit, was obviously there selling. I sucked in my disconcerted surprise and walked over to say hello.

"It's my first time here. How does this work?" I asked.

He looked at me with a "yeah, right" expression on his face and said, smiling, "Yeah, right."

"No, I'm not telling you that to, like, say that I don't do this. I'm really serious. I've never been here before." I pleaded for him to believe me.

I remembered this guy from back home. He used to sing occasionally at one of the Hillcrest coffeehouses with live entertainment. I always thought he had a beautiful voice, kind of high for a man, like George Michael's. He was attractive, but small and thin.

He instructed me to stand around in different parts of the bar and try to make eye contact with people. "Someone is bound to lock eyes with you, and if he does, walk over and say hello. Or they might wave you over, or have a drink sent over to you. The going rate is $150 here. Try not to spend too much time in conversation so that you can be out of here as soon as possible." He looked me up and down and said, "You won't have any trouble here, doll, especially in those pants."

The First Customer

I bought myself a Cape Cod and positioned myself at one end of the bar so that I could observe the crowd. I felt more at ease tucked away in a dark corner, though I realized I needed to make myself visible. I was incredibly relieved that I hadn't spotted anyone else I knew. After about twenty minutes of standing and looking around, I noticed an obese, dark-haired man sitting at the bar who kept looking over at me, then down at his cocktail. I locked eyes with him until he waved me over. I swaggered toward him, bluffing a confident look.

I introduced myself as "Marco." His name was Joe. He said he'd never seen me before. I told him I wasn't from LA and that this was my first time at the bar. He said I looked new. I didn't know what he meant by that, but all of a sudden, I felt embarrassed that I wore skintight black vinyl pants. In the middle of this small-talk conversation, a man walked up to us to greet Joe. He was the owner of the bar. I introduced myself to him as "Tony," immediately realizing, before that second syllable escaped my lips, that I'd made my first hooker faux pas. He gave me an enthusiastic "Nice to meet you, Tony!" squeezing my knee, and continued on to his other owner responsibilities.

I clumsily rambled my way through an explanation for why I told Joe my name was "Marco." He didn't seem to care. I felt like a complete moron. I kept thinking what my San Diego friend said, "Don't spend too much time talking." But, as would be customary of me throughout my career as an escort, I would break all the rules, even ones that were supposed to benefit me.

We became engaged in conversation. He was an artist. Numbers was his hangout. He bought only occasionally but liked that I didn't have that "professional hustler" look, like most of the others. Much later, when I would acquire that look at the bar, I would call it the "Don't even think of bullshitting me" look. Joe had a very gentle, homely look, as if he were the kind of man who, at forty-five, was still living with his mother. I told him I was a writer and was looking to find new ways to support myself. For nearly an hour we talked about writing, living in LA, good movies—I was enjoying myself.

"So . . ." I said to Joe, as a cue to move our conversation to its next logical step.

"What would it cost to have you come to my apartment?" he asked softly, though not nervously, like I would later hear from not-so-regular Numbers customers.

"A hundred and fifty dollars," I said, thankful that my friend had informed me of the market price. I wondered what I might have said otherwise. I wasn't good at driving a hard bargain.

"That seems to be the standard here," he said calmly, and agreed to hire.

We both got up from the bar stools at the same time and walked through the crowd and up the staircase together. I felt a burning heat of stares, as if we were wearing bright neon hats that flashed HOOKER and JOHN, with arrows pointing at our heads.

HIV-Positive Porn Star and Prostitute

[A year and a half later] I met a guy at that fabulous LA den of depravity called the Probe. He had purple spiked hair, piercings in his ears, nipples, and belly button, and a tanned body so perfectly proportioned and defined, he looked as if he'd been skillfully painted into the atmosphere. His unique style in a room full of beauty clones caught my attention. We flirted on and off for about an hour, though his interest in me seemed undecided. After I realized he wasn't interested in hooking up that evening, I went to the bar and wrote on a piece of paper, "You're a beautiful boy," with my phone number. I handed it to him and asked him to call me so I could take him out.

I'd dated only one guy, Gary (for a very short time), in the year and a half since becoming an escort. The week I met him, in the summer of 1997, I was shooting *Positively Yours*, the historic porno flick that was the first to tackle the subject of HIV, with the first ever openly HIV-positive model, myself. While I was proud of these claims to fame, I lied to my new flame by telling him I had family obligations and so, therefore, couldn't see him during the weekend. By this point, dating Tony Valenzuela came to mean surviving my one-two-three punch: HIV-Positive–Porn Star–Prostitute.

Immediately, I felt guilty about lying, so I called Gary back and told him the truth about my porn movie role and then disclosed my HIV status. He, too, was positive and had only slight reservations about seeing a "porn star," but not enough to stop seeing me on the spot. It wasn't until a week later, after deciding that keeping this information from him was misleading, that I revealed my true profession through a carefully crafted e-mail. His reaction was fairly supportive, and he had a million questions about the nature of the business. But soon after, the romance fizzled, and, to this day, I'm not completely sure why, even though Gary and I have become close friends. I never had the guts to come out and say, "So, was it because I'm a hooker?"

Escorts and Dating

Since Gary, I hadn't dated another guy. I'd moved to Los Angeles about a year into my call boy career, which was proving to be financially successful. As much as escorting had become a regular job to me, with a number of great repeat clients whom had genuinely become my friends, and the mindless routine that everyone has in every job, I understood that most people, even gay men, considered the profession contemptible. While I can very well distinguish sex for money from sex with a romantic interest, most guys cannot. Even "open-minded" men draw the line at *dating* an escort. So to save myself the hurt of rejection or insult, I'd closed myself to romance.

But this purple-haired original mesmerized me, and I couldn't resist asking him out. He called me the following afternoon, much to my surprise. We had a pleasant conversation on the phone about his hair stylist career, my activist background, and why I moved to Los Angeles. We made a date to meet that evening for a drink at Marix, an overcrowded Sunday night hangout in West Hollywood. While a part of me was taking the evening casually, another part of me was hopeful. I regretted that dating felt near to impossible for an escort. So why even bother, I fretted.

After arriving at the restaurant and ordering margaritas on the rocks, we found a place to stand and continued the "getting to know you" we'd started on the phone that afternoon. We covered the basics: work, family, drugs, what we thought of each other when we first met at Probe. He told me he actually would not have considered going out with me because I looked like one of those "typical" Probe guys, but that he was impressed by the way I asked him out. "No one says 'I'd like to take you out' anymore," he said. "It's always, 'Here's my number. Call me.'"

"There's a lot about me that's surprising," I said. Over the course of an hour and a half and three strong margaritas, we were having a lovely, almost intimate conversation within the shoulder-to-shoulder confines of Marix. He excused himself to go to the bathroom, and I sat debating when to deliver my one-two-three punch. I could skip the porn star part, I thought. If he can handle HIV and prostitution, he's likely to consider porn a virtue in comparison. But is it necessary to tell him now? Is it inappropriate and presumptuous?

The tequila was swimming through my bloodstream like underwater ballet dancers. I felt warm and contented. I felt like telling him and not having to preoccupy myself between now and date number two with the anxiety of disclosure. After all, at that point, I wasn't that invested, and I was looking for a man in my life who had a broad enough mind and a strong enough character to accept prostitution for what it is—my livelihood.

He came back to our little space, and this is what I said: "You know how you told me your impression of me changed by the way I asked you out? Well, there are some other things

I need to tell you that might seem surprising also, considering what you know about me already."

Telling the Truth

When I'm nervous, and I was terribly nervous, I speak quickly and I ramble. "The first thing is that I'm HIV positive. I've been positive for three and a half years, but I'm healthy, and I take medications, which I'm doing really well on. Some guys aren't comfortable to be with someone who's positive, which I understand, so I wanted you to know that now." I was absorbed in my testimony, more concerned with getting the words out clearly than gauging his response.

I thought we would probably have sex later that night. Not that I always disclose my HIV status before sex, but with the degree of intimacy we were establishing, I didn't want any nasty surprises. I'd recently hooked up with a twenty-four-year-old at the Roxy in New York City. We hadn't even had sex, and when I told him I was HIV positive, he freaked out because we'd been kissing for several hours.

I continued, "About a year and a half ago, I decided I needed to find a way to support myself that allowed me to pursue my goals as a writer. So, what I did was tried out being an *escort*." I emphasized escort so he would understand the broader context under which I was using the word. "And it worked out really well. So, that's how I make my living. While I do all those other things I've told you about, like writing and activism, my main source of income is as an escort." I hated feeling like I needed to counter my "good" qualities with the "vice" of my profession.

Throughout my confessional, he stared at me with an expression that looked neither accepting nor critical. I took in a breath and said, "That's it. . . . *Sooo* . . ." I laughed nervously.

He paused for a moment, then began, "I told you my impression of you switched by the way you asked me out. Well, it's completely switched back to what I first thought of you." I was taken aback by his sharp tone. "Do you really expect that I would go out with you knowing what you just told me? I mean, the HIV part I understand because I think you should say something. But the escort part? Doesn't that just mean male prostitute?"

I was stunned at his almost cruel delivery, though un-flinching and calm in my response, "Yes it does. You know, I don't expect anyone to go out with me knowing I'm an escort, but I do conceive of the idea of guys existing who would."

I saw our date spiraling downward in a fiery ball. I was wondering if I would have to walk home or if he would still drive me home after this confrontation. But all of a sudden, as blunt as his initial reaction had been, his tone softened.

"I said to you earlier that I'm not a judgmental person." He was referring to our discussion about drugs and how he doesn't generally use them, but doesn't care if others do. "It's all okay with me, everything you just told me. It's all fine." He grabbed my knee and smile.

Learning to Trust Others

I didn't understand what had just occurred in his head to in-spire his change of heart. His temperament seemed humble now. With such an instantaneous turnaround in opinion, I thought he'd remembered something in his own past that smacked him in the face with hypocrisy. But I was speculat-ing, and I didn't feel like asking. Several days later, when I did ask about his "360" turn in opinion, he apologized, admitting he was shocked by my news. He told me he just as quickly re-solved that he wasn't going to let his prejudices intercept what might be meeting a "great" person.

It's interesting the trust you gain from people when you divulge sensitive personal information. The first-date insecuri-ties that kept us from touching each other in a demonstrative fashion melted away. After taking the conversation in a lighter direction for a while, we left Marix holding hands and headed for Mickey's.

Some people might think I should not have tolerated his initial condemnation. But I felt like I'd told him something truly unexpected and out of the ordinary. I was, by then, used to accommodating others for my peculiar life's experiences by cutting them some slack, but only at first. Everyone deserves a chance to prove their character.

At one point, a couple of hours later, while we were on the dance floor at Mickey's, he stopped, looked me in the eyes, and said, "You were incredible back at the restaurant, being so completely honest with me."

I will never forget those words. Regardless of whether I dated him for only a short time or ended up marrying him, in one sentence, he gratified the intense labor of honesty I've ventured to pursue, not only with him, but throughout my life. It's odd and amazing to me how such a small gesture of understanding made me feel like bursting into tears. I contained my emotions and hugged him, kissing his neck.

A Former Prostitute Finds God

Shelley Lubben

Shelly Lubben was introduced to sex and alcohol at an early age, and had left home by age eighteen. On her own, she quickly became involved in prostitution, living a dangerous lifestyle. She became pregnant three times and eventually had a child. Lubben also became addicted to alcohol and drugs, worked in the adult film industry, and was so unhappy with her life that she attempted to commit suicide. After meeting a love interest, however, she remembered her Christian roots, and her life slowly started to improve. She quit working as a prostitute, joined a recovery program, and had another daughter. Because of her experience, Lubben now works as an activist to help others within the prostitution and the adult film industries.

I was born in 1968 and grew up in Southern California. I am the eldest of three children and was born a strong-willed child with a "spirited" personality. The first 8 years of life my family attended a good church where I learned about God and Jesus. As a little girl, I knew and loved Jesus very much.

When I turned 9 years old things changed in our family. We moved to Glendora and left the church and friends we knew and loved. My parents stopped attending church and our family drifted away from God and each other. I grew up not having much of a relationship with either of my parents, although they were not bad people. Much of our family time was spent sitting in front of the television. Our family loved to watch television. I still remember most of the episodes from the 70's and 80's shows. I watched a lot of television and

Shelley Lubben, "Former Porn Actress and Prostitute," *ShelleyLubben.com*, October 2007. Reproduced by permission.

111

from it began to develop wrong and harmful thinking. My mother always said the TV was the best babysitter.

Growing up, I was different than other kids. I was highly creative and writing poetry and short stories at a young age. I was very frustrated because I had no place to channel my creative energy. My parents didn't involve me in extracurricular activities and most of the time I was very bored. At 6 years old, I wrote, directed, produced and "starred" in plays I put on at my school. My first grade teacher saw the creativity in me. She told my mother that she was amazed by me and she wanted to see where I was when I was in my 30's. She believed I would become a Hollywood actress or movie producer.

An Early Introduction to Sex

I was also peculiar in the fact that I began masturbating and had sexual tendencies at a very young age. I was sexually abused by a girl and her teenage brother when I was 9 years old and from then on had several sexual encounters with both girls and boys before age 18. Sex became confusing to me. Sex meant "love" to me as it felt good to be wanted by someone and receive attention but at the same time I felt dirty. I didn't recognize until later that I had been sexually violated as a child.

As a teenager, I looked for love in boys and alcohol and started having sex at age 16. My teenage years were filled with constant yelling and arguing between my parents and I. I had a mother who was often mad at me and a father who seemed too busy to have a relationship with me other than yelling at me for talking back to my mother. I don't remember anyone saying "I love you" during those years. My parents weren't bad people but I felt they didn't take much interest in me and I became a rebellious, resentful teenager who acted out to get attention. But instead of getting their attention, my parents preferred to maintain peace in the home. So I was allowed to do things like dress up as a playboy bunny at age 15. I was allowed to date boys they didn't know. At 15 I was allowed to go to a prom with an 18 year old boy who got me drunk for the first time. This began a lifestyle of partying for me and I started hanging out at nightclubs using drugs at 16. My parents knew I had alcohol problems but they didn't know what to do with me. They attempted family counseling but my father was "busy" working and only came once. So I went searching for a new family and found "love" in the wrong crowd, drinking alcohol regularly and getting high on marijuana. My parents went through a lot of anguish because of my actions, and finally—being at their wits end—told me to leave home at age 18.

I ended up in the San Fernando Valley with no food and no money. A "nice" man saw I was upset and told me how sorry he was. He put his arm around me and consoled me and then offered to help me. But then he told me he knew a man who wanted to have sex with me and he'd give me money. I was still in shock and so full of rage because my parents kicked me out that I didn't care anymore so I accepted his offer. I sold myself for $35 and a life of prostitution began for me.

Living on the Edge

Before long I met a madam who introduced me to the "glamorous" side of prostitution. She taught me every trick of the trade and how to manipulate men. At first it seemed exciting with men giving me money, jewelry and gifts but soon it became a life of slavery. I found myself having bizarre sex with strangers and began to hate it. Clients would do things like break condoms on purpose or follow me around and stalk me. One man tried to kill me and hit me with his truck. Another man carried a gun whenever he was with me and threatened to kill me if I didn't perform certain sex acts. Men made demands on me and I was constantly having to lie in order to get out of very frightening situations. I became a professional liar and could literally lie my way out of anything. I even lied my way out of several DUI's and several near death experiences. This is the standard for the sex industry and is the main survival tool for any stripper, prostitute or porn actress.

The sex industry lifestyle was getting worse and worse for me and I felt like I had no where to turn. Jesus kept tugging at my heart but I ignored Him. I figured, God wasn't taking care of me so I had to do what ever I could to survive.

This vicious cycle of working as a prostitute and exotic dancer in Southern California lasted for eight years. While working as a prostitute, I became pregnant three times from clients and it devastated me. A million questions formed in my mind each time. How could I let this happen? How would I take care of the baby? Should I have an abortion? Where could I turn to? I didn't even know who the fathers were for two of the pregnancies. Then I remembered Jesus and I begged Him, "Please help me". God comforted me and I knew I could never kill a life so I kept my baby. Two of the pregnancies ended in miscarriage but one of them did not and I had my first daughter, Tiffany, at age 20. She is mixed with Asian and is very beautiful. I tried to go back to doing only exotic dancing, but prostitution crept up on me and was hard to resist, especially as a single mother.

After a few years as a single mother and working as a prostitute and dancer, I began to drink very heavily and developed a terrible addiction to alcohol and drugs. Tiffany grew up a sad little girl neglected and her innocence was often violated. As she grew older she realized strange men were "visiting" me and was angry with me. I use to make her hide in her bedroom while I "entertained" clients. She also saw me in "peculiar" relationships with women. She didn't totally understand it all but she definitely was subjected to living with a lewd wild woman. I was such a bad mother, that I used to give Tiffany a beeper and make her go to the park while I pulled tricks. She was only four years old.

Making Adult Films

I began to see myself as a complete failure. I lost all self worth and hated myself for being a horrible mother. I was so tired from always trying to survive. There was never any rest from the lifestyle. Men followed me home, slashed my tires, called me at all hours, came over drunk in the middle of the night, and even attempted to kill me. To function, I always had a big bottle of Jack Daniels on hand. Sometimes I'd go sit in a corner with my bottle and cry out totally drunk to Jesus, "Please help me!", but it seemed He wasn't there. Yet I always felt a strange "protection" around me.

As my painful journey progressed, I became involved in the adult film industry. I learned I could make quick easy money and it seemed safer and more legal than prostitution. Many of the prostitutes I knew were getting raped and sent to jail and I didn't want that to happen to me. Also by this time I was a hardcore alcoholic and drug user and pretty incapable of making rational decisions.

When I did my first adult film something very "dark" came over me. I could almost hear the devil say, "See Shelley, I will make you famous and THEN everyone will love you." A powerful strange force enabled me to perform at intense levels only to come off the high and find myself shattered from the shame and degradation. I loved the attention but hated myself at the same time. I loved to hear how great I was but hated the brutal sex. I began to do very hardcore movies and only more drugs and alcohol could get me through them. It was like I had something to prove to the world and to everyone who had ever hurt me. And when the porn industry opened their big arms to me and invited me into their "family", I finally found acceptance. But the price I paid for family "membership" was the price of my own life. I sold what was left of my heart, mind and femininity to the porn industry and the woman and person in me died completely on the porn set.

I also risked becoming infected with the AIDS virus like other porn stars did. I played a crazy and deadly game of Russian roulette with my life. The industry did not and still does NOT enforce condom usage so STD's and HIV were and are still a risk among porn actors and actresses. In May 2004, the Adult Industry Medical Foundation (AIM), which offers monthly voluntary testing of porn performers for HIV, announced that five pornography "actors" had tested positive for the AIDS virus. I was luckier than those actors. God had spared me from contracting HIV. I did however catch herpes, a non-curable sexually transmitted disease. I wanted to end my life. At the time I caught herpes, I had no help and no one to help me deal with the disease. But since AIM came on the scene, the organization claims to have lowered some of the spread of HIV in the adult industry and increased awareness among performers. But the truth remains, porn actors continue to risk their lives and spread disease. In an interview on Court TV with AIM founder, Sharon Mitchell, also former porn actress, admitted that among porn actors today there are "7% HIV, and 12–28% STDs. Herpes is always about 66%. People are medicated with acyclovir for herpes, which is very effective in preventing the herpes outbreaks. Chlamydia and gonorrhea, however, along with hepatitis, seem to stick to everything from dildos to flat surfaces to hands, so, pardon my expression, but we are usually up to our asses in chlamydia.". . .

Leaving the Porn Industry

I swallowed a number of prescription pills and sliced my wrists but it seemed no matter what I did, I couldn't die. The pain was overwhelming and I had terrible mood swings. One minute I walked around like a zombie and then the next minute I'd throw fits of rage, yelling and breaking things. I was mad at God, hated myself and hated my parents. Only alcohol and drugs could soothe my pain. I cried out to Jesus to help me and tried to give up the lifestyle but within a week I'd be back in the vicious cycle. I lost all hope and hated my life. I was completely hopeless and life was utterly meaningless. After becoming infected with herpes, I quietly left the porn industry but went back to prostitution to survive.

In 1994 I met a man named Garrett. He was 22 years old and innocent compared to me. I told him I charged money to date. He pretended to need my "services" for a bachelor party so I gave him my card. He called me often to go out but I kept saying no. I wasn't able to have a normal relationship because my heart was completely black and cold toward all men. Later on though, for some GOD reason, I changed my mind and went out with him. We became friends instantly. As we spent time together, my broken black heart started to feel again. I remember feeling actual physical pain in my heart when Garrett tried to get close to me. (Watch the end of the Grinch movie when his heart started to grow and that was me.)

I tried to keep the relationship distant but it was hard because Garrett made me feel like a little girl again. He'd come over and we'd get high on meth and play checkers and cards for hours. We were like two little kids having fun. I hadn't had "fun" since I was a little girl. Garrett and I would talk about everything and one day we both brought up Jesus. Both of us grew up as kids loving and knowing Jesus Christ. I learned that Garrett was raised in a Christian home and grew up attending Christian school. For two people who met at a bar, this was an amazing "coincidence". I opened up about the trauma I had been through and he was there for me. He knew I did porn and was a prostitute but he felt so bad for me. He said he wanted to rescue me. I never met any man like Garrett. He saw something in me no one else did. He was a friend to a prostitute, just like Jesus. We knew God was working in our lives so we turned back to Jesus and got married on February 14, 1995.

Our new life together began as a total disaster. Garrett lost his job after we were married because he was high on drugs at work. We had to go on welfare and receive financial help. Everything got worse and the temptation for me to go back to the old lifestyle was overwhelming. But God had a better idea. Garrett joined the Army.

Asking for Forgiveness

After basic training, Garrett returned a new man, free from drug addiction and on his way to Fort Lewis military base in Washington state. I became pregnant and gave birth to our daughter, Teresa, in 1997. I was able to quit drinking during the pregnancy but soon went back to alcohol.

Every time I held my new baby, I was reminded how utterly rejected I felt by my parents and all the men and women who abused me. God allowed me to feel the deep pain so He could heal me but I couldn't handle that pain. I grabbed alcohol instead. But the pain was getting worse so I went for counseling at the Army mental health clinic and was diagnosed with Bipolar Disorder, Impulse Control Disorder, Alcohol Dependence, Depressive Disorder and Post Traumatic Stress Disorder. I was prescribed Zoloft, sleeping pills, lithium and counseling. I was given anger management videos to watch which only made me more angry! I went through the Army's substance abuse program but still drank. I was also diagnosed with early cervical cancer and told I needed to have surgery. The consequences of my past were catching up with me. I wanted to give up. Nothing was working!! But God had a better plan.

God led Garrett and I to attend an awesome church called Champions Centre in Tacoma, Washington where we were taught how to live a champion life. The church is known for building Champions for life through the wisdom of God's Word. I was taught how to live a life where I could overcome ANYTHING because with God ALL THINGS ARE POSSIBLE.

With God, I had true forgiveness from all my sins and a chance to grow into a whole new person without being perfect first. That was a relief! I learned that God loved me unconditionally, regardless of my past, and even had a plan for my future. God had a plan for my life? It was like someone turned the light on for me.

In November, 1999, I gave birth to our daughter, Abigail, and though I drank alcohol during part of the pregnancy, God spared her life. After she was born, God FINALLY answered my prayers and took my alcohol addiction away. I began sobriety on April 9, 2000, and it was a very special time in my life. I started to hunger to know God more and to learn everything about being a "normal" woman. I started reading books on how to be a great mom and wife and how to cook and take care of my home. I watched other women to learn how they did laundry, how they dressed, how they talked to their husbands and their kids. I was a perpetual EAVESDROPPER for many years. I would be standing in the meat section of the grocery store and listen to the lady next to me describe how to cook a pot roast and then I'd run home and try it! I hung out in the grocery store just to learn!! Literally, I probably have over 100 mentors who don't even know how much they helped me. I had to start ALL OVER from scratch and learn how to be a normal person living in a normal society and so I began to surround myself with excellent people to learn from them.

Battling Addictive Behavior

I also practiced God's principles in everything I did and began to experience real joy for the first time in 13 years!! God also helped me learn web design so I could have a sense of accomplishment and use my creativity. I owned and operated my own web design business for 4 years. I also began attending college and am near completion for my Bachelor's in Theology degree.

Because I chose to follow Him wholeheartedly, He blessed everything I touched just like His Word promises:

John 13:17 Now that you know these things, you will be blessed if you do them.

After walking in that first day to the Champion center broken and shattered, eight years later I walked out a Champion woman healed and excited to live life! God totally restored me from drugs, alcohol addiction, painful memories, mental illness, sexual addiction, sexual trauma, and the guilt and shame from my past. God took me out of the old life, offered me a new life, and though I couldn't see it in the beginning, I put my hand in His and took a chance on Him. That was the best choice I ever made!

God also restored my femininity and healed my sexuality, which is a major miracle for me. After doing prostitution and porn I lost ability to function sexually. The fact that I can enjoy a healthy sexual relationship now is an absolute miracle. God also healed me of the non-curable disease herpes. I was part of a special military study for pregnant women with herpes in 1996 and when I was tested they said I couldn't be in the study because there was no herpes virus in my blood. The test came back negative! I also am cancer free as the doctors were able to remove all the cervical cancer. He's Jehovah-Rophe the God that heals us!

God also healed our marriage in a remarkable way. Garrett and I have a beautiful and loving relationship that sizzles!. . .

God has done many other miracles in my family as well. Garrett has a great job so I am able to stay home and be a mommy and do ministry. Our three Champion daughters are being raised with the knowledge of Jesus Christ and they attend Christian schools. My eldest daughter Tiffany, who is now 18, has forgiven me and allows me to be a Mother to her. She has overcome many things in her life and now shares her story with others to inspire and encourage them. I am SO thankful I didn't have an abortion because Tiffany is a beautiful brilliant young woman with so much to offer. She is very gifted musically and plays several instruments. Tiffany also feels called by God to reach out to hurting teens. . . . Her desire is to attend college and earn a counseling degree so she can use her past experiences and an education to reach out to teens who struggle.

Rescuing Girls
from Prostitution

Somaly Mam, as told to John Follain

In an interview with John Follain, Somaly Mam explains that she knows about the ravages of prostitution firsthand: after she shot her abusive husband in the foot, he sold her to a brothel. Because of her experience, Mam operates a shelter for girls who have been rescued from prostitution. Removing girls from pimps and brothels, however, has often placed her in danger; in one instance, a man put a gun to her head. Mam finds her job difficult; she is frustrated by political corruption and she dislikes meeting with politicians and donors. She feels little joy in life and has attempted to commit suicide, but seeing the girls at the shelter helps her to continue her work.

"I wake with the sound of birds at 5. As soon as I open my eyes I think of the things I have to sort out. I have a shower, no breakfast. I get lunch for my children, then spend time on e-mails before setting out at 7. My house isn't far from Phnom Penh [Cambodia], but the drive can last five minutes or half an hour, depending on the rain and the state of the road.

I go first to our shelter where the girls we've rescued live. They can be hard to manage—they want to break everything—but I take them in my arms and we understand each other. In Cambodia, parents sell their children when they're five or six for as little as £60. Girls prostitute themselves for less than £1.

It's what I've been through that gives me the strength to fight back. I don't know who my parents are. As a child I remember being cold all the time. I was abandoned and raped when I was 12. Two years later I was sold off and forced to

John Follain, "Interview: A Life in the Day: Somaly Mam," *Times Online*, December 4, 2005. Copyright © 2005 by John Follain/NI Syndication Limited. Reproduced by permission.

marry. My husband would get drunk, he beat me and raped me, he'd fire bullets which passed just by my head or my feet. I took the gun and shot him in the foot. I was 15. I didn't want to kill him, just hurt him as he had hurt me. I'm more of a Buddhist now, and I try to be reasonable. But when I see rapists I see red. I'm not perfect.

My husband sold me to a brothel. I had to accept five or six clients a day. Once a client called me and another girl; he said he was with just one other man. In fact, there were 20 of them; they treated us so badly I wanted revenge. I wanted to kill the man who called us. Then I thought his family would suffer, so I left him alone.

The Harsh Realities of Prostitution

People laugh about prostitution being the oldest job in the world, but I've seen so many awful things. Girls are chained up and beaten with electric cables; one had a nail driven into her skull for trying to escape. Another, Thomdi, was sold to a brothel when she was nine. When I saw her in the street she was 17 and sick with AIDS and TB. She had lots of abscesses and the people at the hospital insulted her and refused to take her in. So I took her home and washed her. She started to get better. Then I had to go abroad. She told me she would die without me, but I had to go. I was buying presents for her when I got the call that she had died. I still feel guilty about her death.

Around mid-morning I go to the offices. I'm back on the computer and I check on the girls' health, and how they are doing at their jobs. The association has a staff of 134, including doctors, psychologists and teachers. Since we set it up eight years ago, we've saved over 3,000 girls and found them normal work.

Our job is dangerous. Once this man who ran a brothel put a gun to my temple; he was angry that I'd talked to his girls. He told me I was a bitch, that he was going to kill me. I talked to him—I knew he wouldn't kill me. People with a gun kill you or they don't—they don't pretend. After, I got him arrested. I don't have bodyguards—I want to be free.

For me, meeting a politician or a donor is much worse than having a gun pointed at me. I didn't go to school, I don't find it easy to talk and behave properly with a bureaucrat. I have to say the truth, which hurts, but if you don't tell the truth, nothing changes.

I'm usually too busy to have lunch, but if I eat something it'll be boiled white rice and fried vegetables. Around 2pm, we hold meetings, we talk about the girls who are ill or have difficulty finding a place in society. And there are always e-mails—I get 200 to 300 a day.

Fighting a Corrupt System

The hardest thing for me to cope with is corruption. I filmed a police raid on a brothel—there was cocaine there. But then in the courts the judge said it wasn't cocaine, it was flour. We once caught a German paedophile on camera, but the courts let him off with a £4,000 fine. He went back to his country. Is that fair?

Last December we rescued 89 women and children in a police raid on a big hotel. But the pimps went to our shelter and grabbed them back. The next day they threatened to come back with grenades. I phoned everyone I could for help, but I was told I'd gone too far—I had bothered powerful people. I make a point of going to see the criminals who threaten me. I have to show them I'm not afraid by talking to them.

I get desperate at times; I tried to commit suicide two or three times. When things are overwhelming, I try to be alone somewhere dark and quiet. I can be bad company; everything makes me angry. I'm separated from my husband and I don't think I'll have another relationship. I'm not young any more; I don't want to make a man unhappy.

One or two nights a week I meet girls in brothels or on the streets. I talk to them and tell them what we could do for them. But usually I go home at 7 to cook for my children. They are in bed by 10, then it's quiet and I go back to my e-mails.

I can be at the computer until 2am.

I don't sleep well. Especially when I have to meet journalists and they ask me about my past. When I close my eyes I feel raped and dirty. I'm very weak. At night when I don't sleep, I think that right at that moment many children are being raped. The pills I used to take don't work any more. But I can get by with two or three hours' sleep. I don't know what being happy means. But I like seeing the girls smile. That makes me feel good.

Organizations to Contact

The editors have compiled the following list of organizations concerned with the issues debated in this book. The descriptions are derived from materials provided by the organizations. All have publications or information available for interested readers. The list was compiled on the date of publication of the present volume; the information provided here may change. Be aware that many organizations take several weeks or longer to respond to inquiries, so allow as much time as possible.

The Alan Guttmacher Institute
120 Wall St., 21st Fl., New York, NY   10005
(212) 248-1111 • fax: (212) 248-1952
e-mail: info@guttmacher.org
Web site: www.guttmacher.org

The institute works to protect and expand the reproductive choices of all women and men. It strives to ensure that people have access to the information and services they need to exercise their rights and responsibilities concerning sexual activity, reproduction, and family planning. The institute publishes the following bimonthly journals: *Perspectives on Sexual and Reproductive Health, International Family Planning Perspectives*, and the *Guttmacher Report on Public Policy*. Selected articles from these publications, including "Ominous Convergence: Sex Trafficking, Prostitution, and International Family Planning" and "Global Concern for Children's Rights: The World Congress Against Sexual Exploitation," are available on its Web site.

American Civil Liberties Union (ACLU)
125 Broad St., 18th Fl., New York, NY   10004-2400
(212) 549-2500
e-mail: aclu@aclu.org
Web site: www.aclu.org

The ACLU champions the human rights set forth in the U.S. Constitution. It works to protect the rights of all Americans and to promote equality for women, minorities, and the poor. The ACLU opposes the U.S.AID requirement that public health organizations and other groups that receive funding under the AIDS Leadership Act must adopt a written policy "explicitly opposing prostitution and sex trafficking." The organization publishes a variety of handbooks, pamphlets, reports, and newsletters, including the quarterly *Civil Liberties* and the monthly *Civil Liberties Alert*. The article "Global AIDS Gag Holds Critical Funding Captive to Politics," is available on its Web site.

Captive Daughters
3500 Overland Ave., Suite 110–108
Los Angeles, CA   90034-5696
fax: (310) 815-9197
e-mail: mail@captivedaughters.org
Web site: www.captivedaughters.org

The mission of Captive Daughters is to end the sexual bondage of female adolescents and children. Its goal is to educate the public about the worldwide problem of sex trafficking and to promote policies and action to prevent it. Its Web site publishes an annotated bibliography of books and films and previously published articles, including "Sex Trafficking: The Real Immigration Problem."

Coalition Against Trafficking in Women (CATW)
PO Box 9338, N. Amherst, MA   01059
fax: (413) 367-9262
e-mail: info@catwinternational.org
Web site: www.catwinternational.org

CATW is a nongovernmental organization that promotes women's human rights. It works internationally to combat sexual exploitation in all its forms, especially prostitution and trafficking in women and children. CATW publishes articles, reports, and speeches on issues related to sex trafficking, including "On the Battlefield of Women's Bodies: An Overview of the Harm of War to Women" and "The Case Against the Legalization of Prostitution," which are available on its Web site.

Concerned Women for America (CWA)

1015 Fifteenth St. NW, Suite 1100, Washington, DC   20005
(202) 488-7000 • fax: (202) 488-0806
e-mail: mail@csfa.org
Web site: www.cwfa.org

CWA works to strengthen marriage and the traditional family according to Judeo-Christian moral standards. It opposes abortion, pornography, homosexuality, and the legalization or decriminalization of prostitution. The organization publishes numerous brochures and policy papers as well as *Family Voice*, a monthly newsmagazine. Selected articles opposing the legalization or decriminalization of prostitution such as "Trafficking of Women and Children" are available on its Web site.

Free the Slaves

1012 Fourteenth Street, NW, Suite 600
Washington, DC   20005
(202) 638-1865 • fax: (202) 638-0599
e-mail: info@freetheslaves.net
Web site: www.freetheslaves.net

Free the Slaves dedicates itself to ending slavery worldwide. It partners with grassroots antislavery organizations and concerned businesses to eradicate slavery from product supply chains and to build a consumer movement that chooses slave-free goods. Free the Slaves also encourages governments to draft and enforce effective antislavery and anti-trafficking laws. The organization publishes reports such as *International Trafficking in Women to the United States: A Contemporary Manifestation of Slavery and Organized Crime*, which is available on its Web site.

Global Rights
1200 Eighteenth Street NW, Suite 602
Washington, DC   20036
(202) 822-4600 • fax: (202) 822-4606
Web site: www.globalrights.org

Global Rights is a human rights advocacy group that partners with local activists worldwide to challenge injustice. The organization opposes U.S. laws that require organizations receiving U.S. global HIV/AIDS and anti-trafficking funds to adopt organization-wide positions opposing prostitution. Global Rights claims that such laws restrict the ability of local activists to prevent the spread of AIDS and to advocate for the health and human rights of women and men in prostitution. It publishes the quarterly magazine *VOICES*, and news, reports, and analysis on trafficking. Articles such as "Slavery in Our Midst: The Human Toll of Trafficking" are available on its Web site.

Human Rights Watch
350 Fifth Ave., 34th Fl., New York, NY   10118-3299
(212) 290-4700
e-mail: hrwnyc@hrw.org
Web site: www.hrw.org

Founded in 1978, this nongovernmental organization conducts systematic investigations of human rights abuses, including sex trafficking, in countries around the world. It publishes many books and reports on specific countries and issues as well as annual reports, recent selections of which are available on its Web site.

International Justice Mission (IJM)
PO Box 58147, Washington, DC   20037-8147
(703) 465-5495 • fax: (703) 465-5499
e-mail: contact@ihm.org
Web site: www.ijm.org

IJM is a human rights agency that rescues victims of violence, sexual exploitation, slavery, and oppression. Its goals include rescuing victims, bringing accountability under the law to perpetrators, preventing future abuses, and helping victims transition to new lives. IJM publishes articles, reports, and books, including *Terrify No More*, which documents IJM's raids in the Cambodian village of Svay Pak, where its workers rescued thirty-seven underage victims of sex trafficking, many of them under the age of ten.

International Sex Worker Foundation for Art, Culture, and Education (ISWFACE)

801 Cedros Ave., No. 7, Panorama City, CA   91402
(818) 892-2029
e-mail: iswface@iswface.org
Web site: www.iswface.org

ISWFACE is an organization run by current and retired sex workers. It serves as an educational resource center for information about and research on prostitution and sex work. Its goal is to foster, perpetuate, and preserve an appreciation of the art and culture created by and about sex workers. Other goals include educating the public about sex workers, their art, and their culture; providing economic alternatives and opportunities for creative, artistic sex workers; and offering accurate, timely information about sex work to health care and law enforcement organizations.

Polaris Project

PO Box 77892, Washington, DC   20013
(202) 547-7990 • fax: (202) 547-6654
e-mail: info@polarisproject.org
Web site: www.polarisproject.org

The Polaris Project is a multicultural grassroots organization combating human trafficking and modern-day slavery. Based in the United States and Japan, it brings together community members, survivors, and professionals to fight trafficking and slavery. The project's goals include empowering trafficking survivors and effecting long-term social change to end trafficking.

Prostitution Research and Education (PRE)

PO Box 16254, San Francisco, CA 94116-0254
e-mail: contact1@prostitutionresearch.com
Web site: www.prostitutionresearch.com

PRE is a nonprofit organization whose goal is to abolish the institution of prostitution. PRE also gives voice to those who are among the world's most disenfranchised groups: prostituted/trafficked women and children. Publications include articles and reports on the legal, social, and health implications of prostitution and sex trafficking, including "Prostitution: Where Racism and Sexism Intersect" and "Prostitution, Violence, and Post-Traumatic Stress Disorder," which are available on its Web site.

Shared Hope International

PO Box 65337, Vancouver, WA 98665
1-866-HER-LIFE
e-mail: savelives@sharedhope.org
Web site: www.sharedhope.org

Shared Hope International is a nonprofit organization that exists to rescue and restore women and children in crisis. It establishes places to which trafficked women and children can escape and receive health care, education, and job training. It also identifies areas of victimization to increase public awareness and builds alliances to eradicate human trafficking. Fact sheets and the article "Tracing the History of Sex Trafficking" are available on its Web site.

Women's Commission on Refugee Women and Children

122 East Forty-Second St., 12th Fl.
New York, NY 10168-1289
(212) 551-3088 • fax: (212) 551-3180
e-mail: info@womenscommission.org
Web site: www.womenscommission.org

The commission offers solutions and provides technical assistance to ensure that refugee women, children, and adolescents are protected and have access to education, health services, and livelihood opportunities. It makes recommendations to U.S. and United Nations policy makers and nongovernmental organizations on ways to improve assistance to refugee women and children. Experts conduct field research and technical training in refugee camps and detention centers. On its Web site the commission publishes issues of its semiannual newsletter, *Women's Commission News*, and reports and articles, including "The Struggle Between Migration Control and Victim Protection: The UK Approach to Human Trafficking."

World Vision International
800 West Chestnut Ave., Monrovia, CA   91016
(626) 303-8811
e-mail: newsvision@wvi.org
Web site: www.wvi.org

Established in 1950, World Vision International is a Christian relief and development organization that works for the well-being of all people, especially children. Through emergency relief, education, health care, economic development, and promotion of justice, World Vision's goal is to help communities help themselves. It publishes the quarterly *Global Future* and many reports and articles, many of which are available on its Web site, including "Children's Work, Adult's Play: Child Sex Tourism—The Problem in Cambodia."

For Further Research

Books

Karen Abbott, *Sin in the Second City: Madams, Ministers, Playboys, and the Battle for America's Soul.* New York: Random House, 2007.

Kathleen Barry, *The Prostitution of Sexuality.* New York: NYU Press, 1996.

Vern Bullough and Bonnie Bullough, *Women and Prostitution: A Social History.* New York: Prometheus Books, 1987.

Anne M. Butler, *Daughters of Joy. Sisters of Misery: Prostitutes in the American West. 1865–90.* Champaign: University of Illinois Press, 1987.

Michel Dorais, *Rent Boys: The World of Male Sex Trade Workers.* Montreal, Quebec: McGill-Queen's University Press, 2005.

James Elias, Vern L. Bullough, Veronica Elias, and Gwen Brewer, eds., *Prostitution: On Whores, Hustlers, and Johns.* New York: Prometheus Books, 1998.

Melissa Farley, *Prostitution and Trafficking in Nevada: Making the Connections.* San Francisco: Prostitution Research & Education, 2007.

———, ed., *Prostitution, Trafficking and Traumatic Stress.* Binghamton, NY: Haworth Maltreatment and Trauma Press, 2004.

R. Bard Flowers, *The Prostitution of Women and Girls.* Jefferson, NC: McFarland & Company, 1998.

Maria Rosa Henson, *Comfort Woman: A Filipina's Story of Prostitution and Slavery Under the Japanese Military.* New York: Rowman & Littlefield, 1999.

Kamala Kempadoo, ed., *Trafficking and Prostitution Reconsidered: New Perspectives on Migration, Sex Work, And Human Rights*. Boulder, CO: Paradigm Publishers, 2005.

Joanna Phoenix, *Making Sense of Prostitution*. New York: Palgrave Macmillan, 2002.

Nils Johan Ringdal and Richard Daly, *Love for Sale: A World History of Prostitution*. New York: Grove Press, 2004.

Michael Rutter, *Upstairs Girls: Prostitution in the American West*. Helena, MT: Farcountry Press, 2005.

William W. Sanger, *The History of Prostitution: Its Extent, Causes And Effects Throughout the World*. Whitefish, MT: Kessinger Publishing, 2007.

Gene Simmons, *History of Prostitution: A Historical and Personal Perspective of the First and Oldest Profession*. San Francisco: Phoenix Books, 2008.

Jessica Spector, *Prostitution and Pornography: Philosophical Debate About the Sex Industry*. Palo Alto, CA: Stanford University Press, 2006.

Rebecca Whisnant and Christine Stark, eds., *Not for Sale: Feminists Resisting Prostitution and Pornography*. North Melbourne, Australia: Spinifex Press, 2005.

Periodicals

Joyce Adams, "Bring It on Home: Teens and the Real World," *School Library Journal*, April 2007.

Vanessa Baird, "Trafficked: Behind the Doors of Ordinary-Seeming Flats, Houses, Hotels, a Brutal Form of Modern Slavery Is Taking Place," *New Internationalists*, September 2007.

S.M. Berg, "Pornography and Pop Culture: Pornography, Prostitution & Sex Trafficking; How Do You Tell the Difference?" *off our backs*, July 2007.

Christianity Today, "Sex Isn't a Spectator Sport: Germany's World Cup Pimping Will Fuel Sex Trafficking," July 2006.

Kira Cochrane, "Fine Words on a Filthy Trade," *New Statesman (1996)*, October 8, 2007.

Bishakha Datta, "Knowing the Difference: Some Women Sell Sex Voluntarily, Some Are Forced," *New Internationalists*, September 2007.

Melissa Ditmore, "'I Never Want to Be Rescued Again,'" *New Internationalists*, September 2007.

Cyril Doll, "Legal Tricks: Legalized Prostitution Is Promoted as a Women's Rights Issue, But It Simply Legitimizes Sexual Abuse," *Western Standard*, January 29, 2007.

Economist, "Indecent Proposals; Prostitution and Advertising," November 3, 2007.

Clayton Goodwin, "Hi, Dearie, You Want Business? An Influx of African Prostitutes, More a Tide than a Trickle, within the Last Two to Three Years Has Transformed the Appearance and Practice of the Trade in the UK," *New African*, April 2007.

Kerry Howley, "Invasion of the Prostitots: Another Moral Panic About American Girls," *Reason*, July 2007.

Victor Malarek, "Meet the Traffickers: What Kind of Person Would Sell Another? You Might Be Surprised," *New Internationalists*, September 2007.

Timothy C. Morgan, "Sex Isn't Work," *Christianity Today*, January 2007.

New Internationalists, "Stop Traffick! A Global Selection of Some of the More Progressive, Inventive and Even Unusual Initiatives that Have Been Launched to Tackle Trafficking . . . ," September 2007.

Michael Parker, "India's Other Virus: How One Victim Makes a Difference," *UN Chronicle*, September-November 2006.

Margot Patterson, "Hard Truths About Prostitution," *National Catholic Reporter*, February 23, 2007.

————, "Soul Sisters: Former Prostitutes Tell Their Stories to the Women Who Helped Them Leave the Sex Trade," *National Catholic Reporter*, February 23, 2007.

Sandy Fertman Ryan, "Little Girls Lost: This Summer, Hundreds of Thousands of Girls Will Run Away from Home and Become Victims of Horrific Circumstances," *Girl's Life*, June-July 2007.

Jeremy Schneider, "The Men of Boystown: A Glimpse into the World of Male Prostitution," *Christianity Today*, November 2007.

Mary Lucille Sullivan, "Whose Rights Are We Talking About?" *Arena Magazine*, April-May 2007.

Western Standard, "Happier Hookers: The Oldest Profession Poses New Challenges," April 23, 2007.

Index